Italian

Italian

The food and the music

Bath · New York · Singapore · Hong Kong · Cologne · Delhi · Melbourne

This edition published in 2009

Parragon
Queen Street House
4 Queen Street
Bath BA1 1HE, UK

Produced by Terry Jeavons & Company

ISBN 978-1-4075-4837-1

Printed in China

Notes for the Reader
This book uses imperial, metric, and U.S. cup measurements. Follow the same units of measurement
throughout; do not mix imperial and metric. All spoon measurements are level; teaspoons are assumed
to be 5 ml and tablespoons are assumed to be 15 ml. Unless otherwise stated, milk is assumed to be
whole, individual vegetables such as potatoes are medium, and pepper is freshly ground black pepper.
Recipes using raw or very lightly cooked eggs should be avoided by infants, the elderly, pregnant
women, convalescents, and anyone suffering from an illness. Pregnant and breastfeeding women are
also advised to avoid eating peanuts and peanut products. The times given are an approximate
guide only. Preparation times differ according to the techniques used by different
people and the cooking times may also vary from those given.

contents

part three: SECONDI PIATTI

3 meat, poultry, game, fish & seafood, vegetable main courses

introduction

This book is a comprehensive guide to choosing, preparing, and cooking Italian food. Lovers of Italian food will be pleased to find their favorite, classic dishes in addition to a number of new, imaginative recipes in one volume.

The front of the book is packed with information on Italy's favorite ingredients, essential tips for making and cooking perfect pasta and risotto, kitchen equipment that will make food preparation easier, along with all the basic recipes. The inspiring collection of recipes that follows caters for every occasion.

Bursting with freshness, color, and flavor, this book will make your mouth water—with such a choice of recipes you'll wonder where to begin. Perhaps the answer is, at the beginning, as the Italians do. A little antipasto to tempt the tastebuds!

the italian way

We may think of Italy as having a national cuisine but, apart from the pasta and pizza that can be found everywhere, there are strong differences from region to region between the top of its boot to the toe. As the climate and terrain change, so too does the cuisine, the enormous variety in which reflects the local produce, specialties, traditions, and economy of each of the regions.

It wasn't until the Unification of Italy in 1861 that each of the individual states, with their own identity, customs, and cuisine, were combined as a single political entity—the Italy that we know today. Over the years, the borders have become more blurred as people have moved around the country, taking their specialties with them, but it is still almost impossible to define Italian cuisine.

Italian cooking was first inspired by the ancient Romans and then influenced by Greek, Byzantine, and Arab invaders. Other influences were Italy's proximity to France and Austria and the produce brought to the country by the traders who sailed the seas. Venice, once the heart of the world's trading empire, was where ships brought cargoes of lemons and oranges from Asia, spinach from Persia, spices from Syria and Turkey, and eggplants from South-East Asia, not forgetting tomatoes from Peru.

In each of Italy's distinctively regional cuisines the local produce is shown great respect. To the Italians, quality and freshness are very important. They learn about food from a very early age—mothers pass down recipes to daughters—centuries-old recipes are still being used, and families guard their recipes jealously. It is wonderful how they have managed to retain their traditions despite the hectic world in which we now live. They enjoy their food and have the ability to turn a simple family meal into a special occasion.

Although these days most products are available all year round and seasonal produce is not an issue, to the Italian cook the seasons are still of the utmost importance. The Italians take great pride in choosing their ingredients and treat their food with respect. There are fruit and vegetable markets in all Italian towns and Italian cooks will not necessarily go there to buy what they have decided to cook that day, but to choose what is fresh and in season—plump figs, juicy oranges, black and white grapes, ripe cherries, small zucchinis with their orange flowers intact, and tiny sweet tomatoes still attached to the vine.

The same principle applies at the fish market—the Italian cook will select plump, bright whole fish, shrimp still wriggling in their shells, everything freshly caught that morning. Since most of the regions of Italy are bordered by sea and there are many freshwater rivers and lakes in the north, there is an abundance of fish, and it is hardly surprising that the Italians are enthusiastic fish eaters. Local fish markets can be found in most towns and who, on a visit to Venice, hasn't visited La Madonna, the bustling fish market near the Rialto Bridge? The sheer beauty of the fish, trays and trays of different shapes and colors, is a sight for sore eyes.

In the colder north, food is richer and heartier. Cows are bred on fresh grass and provide not only beef and veal but also excellent dairy produce, such as butter and Parmesan cheese. There is even a recipe from the north of Italy for beef braised in milk! Many families raise a pig, feeding it on the whey left over from cheesemaking and hence pork, bacon, sausages, salami, and ham are widely eaten. In addition, during the hunting season, game is often on the menu. The north is where rice is grown and is evident in the eating of risotto, and, more importantly, it is also where maize is grown and polenta is eaten.

In fact polenta is a staple diet in northern Italy and Italians from the south refer to northerners as «polentoni» (polenta eaters). Apples are produced on a large scale, together with vegetables such as potatoes, rutabagas, cabbages, cauliflowers, celery, artichokes, asparagus, and beans. In Tuscany the latter are eaten in such large

quantities, in every way imaginable, that the people are known as «Toscani Mangiafagioli» (The Tuscan Bean-eaters). Wild mushrooms and truffles are collected in the fall in the beech and oak woods that are to be found throughout northern and central Italy and are highly sought after—hunters are even required to be licensed. Chicken and lamb are popular in Tuscany, as is calf's liver. The region of Venice is also is famous for its calf's liver, where the liver of calves under a year old is served fried and smothered with onions (fegato alla Veneziana).

Rice is a staple ingredient in the Italian diet and risotti are frequently served.

Although the region of Liguria is in the north, on the west coast, the Mediterranean climate is perfect for the production of garlic, basil, and pine nuts. The coast is also full of olive groves and the oil produced is mild and sweet and considered by many to be the best. It is this oil that is used to make one of north-western Piedmont's most famous dishes, a hot dip known as Bagna Cauda. This is served in a pot, over a burner, and makes an ideal first course or light meal. It is made by heating ¼ pint/150 ml olive oil, 3 oz/85 g butter, and 2 chopped garlic cloves in a pan for 2 minutes, adding two 1¾ oz/50 g cans of drained and finely chopped anchovies and heating gently for 10 minutes, stirring all the time. The dip is served with sticks of raw vegetables such as celery, carrots, asparagus, and zucchinis, and crusty bread, which are dipped into it.

Moving southward toward central Italy, the fertile land produces broccoli and fennel, as well as salad vegetables and herbs. The mountainous area of central Italy is a region of sheep farmers, and lamb, cooked in a variety of ways is usually the main course. Mountain game such as wild boar can be found slightly further south.

Lamb is usually cooked very young—cuts from older animals benefit from slow cooking techniques.

When we reach southern Italy the weather is warmer and this is the area of lighter food. Colorful fruits, such as oranges and lemons, and vegetables, including ripe tomatoes, bell peppers, zucchinis, artichokes, and eggplants, feature strongly, as does the colorful pizza. Pizzas are made throughout the country but it is said that the best are made in Naples and southern Italy. It was the Neapolitans who first used the tomato, brought to Italy by sailors from South America in the sixteenth century, when it was known as the evil golden apple of Eden as it was eaten while still green. The southern Italians let it ripen and turn red in their hot sun before eating. Now it is still their most valued product and is eaten fresh, used in cooked dishes and sauces, canned, puréed, and dried.

Then there are Italy's islands. At the tip of the toe is Sicily, where the cooking is based on rice, couscous, vegetables, fish, and citrus fruits, particularly lemons, which, along with almond trees, grow in great quantity. Sardinia, off Italy's west coast, is where lamb, pork, game, vegetables, and cheese play the key role. Sardinians also have a wide range of bread and cakes, which often contain almonds and citrus fruits.

Globe artichokes are a type of giant thistle, closely related to the cardoon. The part that is eaten is actually the immature flower bud of the plant. Artichokes are immensely popular throughout Italy during their very short season, and most regions have their own recipe. The smaller, younger buds are the most popular, as these can be eaten whole.

Finally, olive trees cover the center and south of Italy and, as a result, olives and olive oil are plentiful, and the whole country has slopes covered in grapevines laden with delicious grapes. It is hardly surprising that Italy is one of the largest olive oil and wine producing countries in the world!

Traditionally, the main meal of the day in Italy is eaten at lunchtime and the average Italian family eats well. There are many courses in an Italian meal but not all are eaten on a regular basis and an everyday lunch is seldom an elaborate affair. It may start with antipasti, the food that comes before the meal. Its name comes from ante, meaning before, and pasto, meaning meal. Although often cold, there are also some hot antipasti and the selection of ingredients used is enormous. The intention is to stimulate the appetite and an antipasto may consist of just a few dishes such as a platter of prosciutto and a bowl of gherkins or olives, a wider selection of antipasti, occasionally a soup or salad, or something more substantial such as Tomato & Mozzarella Bruschetta. In Venice's wine bars antipasti known as cicheti are served.

A first course (il primo) always starts a meal and may consist of pasta, rice, or gnocchi. These may seem rather substantial, but the servings are small and are followed by a simple meat or fish dish without numerous accompaniments.

It is often suggested that the explorer Marco Polo introduced pasta to Italy from China when he returned from his travels there but the Italians, particularly those in the south, were eating pasta long before then. Now it is eaten in almost every region and has become the most commonly eaten Italian dish, although it wasn't actually until the turn of the twentieth century that it became popular.

A light main course (il secondo) traditionally follows the first course. It usually consists of a small portion of meat, poultry, game, or fish or, occasionally, a vegetable dish, accompanied by either a lightly cooked vegetable or a small salad. The main course is not as substantial as it is in many other cuisines and is cooked and served simply so that the full flavor of the food is appreciated. It is seldom covered in a sauce or served with numerous accompaniments.

At the end of an everyday Italian meal, a bowl of fresh seasonal fruit and a platter of local cheeses are usually served but desserts do feature in their cuisine. These are served for Sunday lunch, on special occasions, and at Christmas and Easter. More often their cakes and pastries are eaten at a café with mid-morning or afternoon cups of coffee. Italians are rightly famous for their refreshing ice creams and water ices, to be eaten at any time of day! In the evening, a lighter meal of antipasti, soup, omelet, or a salad may be served. A cup of espresso, the national drink of Italy, settles the digestion and completes the Italian meal.

The Italians have a passion for their food. They say it's what life is all about! Let's hope that the recipes in this book will infect you with their enthusiasm. Buon appetito!

Despite their international reputation as a nation of coffee-drinkers, Italians will probably drink a maximum of three small cups a day.

ingredients in the italian kitchen

Italy has an abundance of wonderful ingredients. The following are those that you will come across most frequently.

CHEESES

There are numerous Italian hard, semi-soft, and fresh cheeses, but these are the most well known and readily available:

Bel Paese, literally translated, means beautiful country and is originally from the beautiful countryside of Lombardy in northern Italy. Made from cow's milk, it is soft and creamy and has a mild flavor. It can be eaten either on its own or used in a variety of cooked dishes.

Fontina is made in the Valle d'Aosta region and it takes its name from Monte Fontina near the Italian town of Aosta. Cheese that does not bear the description «Fontina from the Valle d'Aosta» is not the genuine cheese. It is a semi-soft, full-fat cheese made from cow's milk. It has a delicate, nutty flavor and, because it melts evenly, it is a good cheese for cooking.

Gorgonzola is a blue-veined cheese, originally from the town of that name. It is made from cow's milk and has a buttery flavor. Gorgonzola Piccante has a sharp flavor and Gorgonzola Dolce is, as the name suggests, sweet. It melts well and is therefore often used in Italian sauces and in dishes such as Bleu Cheese Risotto. Torta di San Gaudenzio is a cheese made from layers of Gorgonzola and mascarpone. Dolcelatte is made from a combination of Gorgonzola and Italian cream cheese, and obviously has a milder, creamier flavor.

Mascarpone comes from southern Lombardy and is a soft cream cheese. It is used in desserts such as Tiramisù, Mascarpone Creams, and Sweet Mascarpone Mousse, or can replace cream in sauces.

Mozzarella is a moist, semi-soft cheese molded into spherical shapes. It has very good melting qualities when heated and is an essential ingredient for topping pizzas. It is also eaten fresh in salads, often with tomatoes and basil and drizzled with olive oil. Mozzarella was originally made with buffalo milk, and this variety has a superior flavor and is less rubbery in texture. Avoid mozzarella made outside of Italy as it is no substitute for the genuine product.

Parmesan is probably the most famous Italian cheese. Genuine Parmesan is made in and around the town of Parma and only then can it bear the name Parmigiano Reggiano, indicating that it is true Parmesan. It is used for grating on top of dishes such as pasta, risotto, polenta, and soup, for shaving onto salads, as an ingredient in dishes such as in Lasagna al Forno, and can be eaten in chunks with bread or fruit. Parmesan belongs to a group of cheeses known as grana, meaning hard and grainy. Grana Padano belongs to the same group and is similar to Parmesan but is slightly inferior and less mature. Always buy fresh Parmesan for grating as pre-packed grated varieties do not compare in flavor.

Provolone, from the south of Italy, is recognized by its large pear-shape, covered in wax and hanging from a string. It is a curd cheese made from cow's milk and is sold fresh, or matured and hard, and can be eaten either way or used in cooking. Provola is a smaller version of provolone, as is caciocavallo, which looks like two saddlebags, and burrini, which are provola cheeses with unsalted butter in the center.

Ricotta is a by-product of the whey, rather than the curd of milk. It is not really a cheese, but today whole or skim milk is added to it and it is sold as soft, white cheese. It has a bland flavor and is used to fill pasta and in desserts and tarts, especially in southern Italy and the islands of Sicily and Sardinia.

Taleggio is a semi-soft, cow's milk cheese that comes originally from the northern Italian Alps. It has a mild, sweet flavor and is best eaten when young as it reaches maturity after only six weeks.

PANCETTA

This is salted, spiced belly of pork, rolled into a large sausage shape and available either in one piece or very thinly sliced. When lean and thinly sliced it can be eaten like prosciutto but it is usually sliced or chopped and then fried, and used in savory dishes such as soups, sauces, and stuffings.

PROSCIUTTO

This is the Italian word for ham. Prosciutto cotto is cooked ham and prosciutto crudo is cured ham. Italy's most famous and popular cured ham is prosciutto di Parma and, like most Italian prosciutto, is air-dried for at least 8 months and sometimes for as long as 2 years. Genuine prosciutto di Parma comes from the area around the city of Parma in Emilia-Romagna and is produced from pigs fed on the whey from making Parmigiano Reggiano. It can be identified by the brand burned onto the skin. It is sliced thinly and should be pale red in color, tender, with a sweet, smoky taste. Only salt is added to flavor it. It is traditionally served as antipasti, with melon, or in recipes such as Prosciutto & Figs. Prosciutto di San Danele is another equally good, if not better, Italian cured ham. It is pale pink in color with a delicate flavor.

OLIVE OIL

Olive oil is made by crushing the flesh of olives before they turn black, and extracting the oil. Some of the best oil comes from Liguria—the flavor and texture of the oil becomes more intense the farther south it is produced. The best olive oil should be heavy, a rich green in color, and taste like green olives. Extra virgin olive oil is made

The soft, crumbly texture of Gorgonzola makes it ideal for use in cooking.

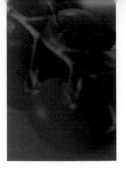

from the first pressing of the olives and is cold pressed, which means that the olives are crushed and the oil extracted without being heated or chemically treated. It has the best flavor and a maximum acidity of 1 percent. Virgin olive oil has an acidity of no more than 1.5 percent; olive oil or pure olive oil is made by using heat and/or pressing to extract the oil and it is then refined. Use your best oil for salads and drizzling over cooked dishes rather than in cooking, where its flavor will be lost and, once a bottle of oil has been opened, use it quite quickly to prevent it going off.

VINEGAR

Red and white vinegars are used in Italian cooking to prepare dressings, sauces, and marinades, as is balsamic vinegar, which is also used sparingly in fish and meat dishes. Balsamic vinegar is made in Modena from sweet white Trebbiano di Spagna grapes by moving the vinegar from successively smaller barrels each year and blending very aged vinegars (up to 100 years old) with younger vinegars (no less than 12 years old). The barrels are manufactured from different aromatic and hard woods, such as old brandy barrels, and these too add flavor to the vinegar as it ages. This produces a rich, dark, syrupy vinegar and its production is protected by a consortium made up of the Modena families who produce it.

Balsamic vinegar between 40 and 50 years old is labeled tradizionale, while vinegar that is 10 or 12 years old is labeled aceto balsamico di Modena.

MARSALA

This is a fortified wine and can be dry, semi-dry, or sweet. It is often used in Italian cooking and is the traditional ingredient in Zabaglione. It is also used in other desserts, such as Marsala Cherries, as well as in savory dishes, particularly veal, pork and some risottos.

CAPERS

These are the little green buds of a low-growing wild shrub. They are an important ingredient in Italian cooking and are used whole or crushed, particularly in fish and veal dishes, sauces, and stuffings. They are available preserved in brine or in vinegar, and those that come from Sicily are traditionally preserved in salt.

ANCHOVIES

Preserved anchovies are an essential ingredient in many Italian dishes, such as Bagna Cauda (see page 12). They are used to flavor sauces and are eaten as an antipasto. They can be found in supermarkets, canned or bottled in either oil or salt, and in delicatessens, preserved just in salt, and they can be whole or filleted. Those preserved in salt must be soaked for 30 minutes, rinsed, and dried well, those canned or bottled in salt must be rinsed, and those preserved in oil should be drained well before use.

PINE NUTS

Umbrella pine trees grow in many parts of Italy but particularly in the Ligurian region in the north west. The nuts are extracted from the seeds found in the pine cones. They have a delicate flavor and are used in stuffings, salads, sprinkled over vegetables, in cookies, cakes, and in pesto sauce. Once opened, do not store for too long as they go off quickly.

CHESTNUTS

These grow in the mountainous areas of Italy and become widely available in the early months of winter. They are used in soups, stews, and sweet dishes as well as being roasted and eaten whole. They are available fresh, vacuum-packed, canned, and frozen.

CEPS

Known in Italy as porcini, these are wild boletus mushrooms. Although available fresh in spring and fall, they are usually bought dried and have a highly concentrated flavor owing to the drying process. They must be soaked in water to reconstitute them before use and are ideal for flavoring risottos, sauces, soups, stuffings, and meat dishes. They can also be added to dishes that contain fresh mushrooms to enhance their flavor.

TOMATOES

This vegetable dominates Italian cooking both as a flavoring and as a vegetable in its own right. Canned chopped tomatoes make an excellent substitute for fresh ones in cooked dishes (a 14 oz/400 g can is equivalent to about 2.4 lb/1 kg fresh tomatoes) and in paste form they are excellent for flavoring dishes. No pantry should be without either.

GARLIC

Garlic is always associated with the cuisine of Italy but, in fact, not all its dishes are highly flavored with it. Its reputation came about because most of the Italian emigrants to Britain and the United States came from southern Italy and more garlic is used in their cooking than anywhere else in Italy.

It is used with discretion in sauces and in meat, fish, and vegetable dishes, and in certain classic dishes that rely on its flavor, such as Green Pesto Sauce.

OLIVES

These are the fruit of an evergreen tree and, depending on the region, the olives in Italy can be large, small, medium-sized, different shades of black or green, pitted or unstoned, stuffed, or tossed in herbs. They are grown both for eating on their own with aperitifs, in antipasti, and in cooking, and for turning into olive oil.

HERBS AND SPICES

Fresh herbs are used in Italian cooking whenever possible. Rosemary is the most popular herb in Tuscany and central Italy and is used to flavor broiled and grilled meat, particularly lamb and chicken. Sage is used mainly in the north in pork dishes and with calf's liver, and flat-leaf parsley is used extensively. Basil is probably the herb most associated with Italian cooking and is a vital ingredient in Green Pesto Sauce, giving it its vibrant green color and distinctive flavor. Along with freshly ground black pepper, the most essential spice in the Italian kitchen is nutmeg. This is always used in spinach and ricotta dishes, both savory and sweet. It should be freshly grated straight into the dish you are preparing.

Mushrooms are a popular ingredient in Italian cooking—the early morning mists of fall bring the mushroom-gatherers out in force, eager to find the best of the day's crop.

«00» FLOUR

This flour is made from Italian soft durum wheat, which produces a strong flour rich in gluten. The wheat is very finely milled to produce «00» grade flour, which is soft and extra fine. It is mostly used to make fresh pasta as it is this high gluten content and the fineness of the flour that gives the pasta its true texture.

PASTA

The national dish of Italy, pasta is made from durum wheat flour, sometimes with the addition of egg and/or oil. It is available in numerous shapes and sizes, from the tiniest shells to large sheets of lasagna, and in different colors and flavors, for example spinach, tomato, beetroot, cuttlefish ink, and herbs. In addition, the names of pasta shapes vary from region to region and from one manufacturer to another. At the last count there were over 650 varieties of pasta shapes. Pasta is available fresh or dried, or you can make it at home (see the Basic Pasta Dough recipe on page 25).

In this book, you will find a selection of pasta recipes served with a sauce. However, if you wish to use a shape of pasta other than the one specified in the recipe, although there are no hard and fast rules, there are some general guidelines, depending on the type of sauce. Short, tubular pasta, twists, and shells, which have hollows and cavities for the sauce to cling to, are best served with chunky, thick sauces such as meat, fish, and vegetable sauces, while long, thin pasta is best served with a simple smooth sauce such as Tomato Sauce or Green Pesto Sauce. The flatter the pasta the richer the sauce it should be eaten with, for example cream or cheese.

Always serve pasta dishes hot, and ideally in deep plates, to keep them warm and prevent any sauce served with them from splashing, and eat with a fork only—never a knife!

Cook's tips for cooking pasta

- Cook in the largest pan that you have in plenty of boiling water.

- Add the pasta to the water only when it is boiling and stir well at the beginning.

- You can add oil to the pasta water to prevent it from sticking, although this is not necessary.

- Cook at a rolling boil.

- Don't over-cook pasta. Dried pasta should still be firm to the bite or «al dente.»

- Don't rinse the cooked pasta.

RICE

Most Italian rice is grown in the north, where rice paddies are part of the land-scape, and is classified by the size of the grain; originario, which is the smallest and is ideal for rice pudding, semifino, which includes varieties such as vialone and nano, fino and superfine, which is the longest and includes the arborio and carnaroli varieties. Only these specialized varieties should be used to make risotto, and each brings its own slightly different texture to the dish. It is the roundness and starchiness of the grain, which swells to at least three times its size while retaining a firm texture during cooking, that makes arborio and carnaroli rice ideal for making risottos. No other variety of rice produces the same soft, creamy texture that is vital for a good risotto.

Cook's tips for cooking risotto

- Use a large shallow pan if possible so that the rice has room to expand.

- Use a wooden, rather than a metal spoon, as it is gentler and prevents damaging the texture of the rice.

- Keep the stock at simmering point so that it is about the same temperature as the rice.

- Stir the rice all the time while cooking, in a clockwise direction, not backward and forward, to prevent damaging the rice.

- Let a risotto stand for 2–3 minutes before serving to allow the flavors of the different ingredients to mingle.

SEMOLINA

This is ground durum wheat, which is available in different size grains. Coarser grains are used to make semolina gnocchi and finer grains are used to make commercial dried pasta as it makes a tough dough that can be forced through dies to form shapes. It can also be used to sprinkle over freshly made pasta dough to prevent it from sticking together.

POLENTA

This is the name given both to an ingredient, which is ground corn, and to an Italian dish, which is a well-known specialty that is particularly popular in northern Italy. There are three varieties of cornmeal available, coarse, medium, and fine, and the coarser the grain the yellower the color. Coarse varieties are used to make polenta and finer varieties are better in cakes. Polenta is made by boiling it with water, stirring constantly for 40 minutes, to make a stiff

porridge. Instant polenta, which takes about 5 minutes to prepare, and ready-to-eat polenta are now available in supermarkets. Polenta has a bland flavor and is usually served with a strong-flavored food or sauce or has ingredients added to it while it is cooking. It can also be fried or grilled after it has been turned out and become cold.

equipment for italian cooking

A basically equipped kitchen is all you need for Italian cooking but, apart from a set of sharp knives, wooden spoons, and a large pan for cooking pasta, there are some specialized pieces of equipment that make food preparation quicker and less demanding. You might consider purchasing some of the following pieces of equipment if you think that you might find them useful.

CITRUS ZESTER
This small tool removes the zest of citrus fruit in long shreds without removing any bitter white pith. The zest is used for flavoring and decorating desserts and cakes.

GARLIC PRESS
Choose a good quality press for crushing the flesh and extracting the juice rather than chopping the garlic by hand.

ICE CREAM MAKER
These vary enormously in style and price but are worth investing in if you make a lot of ice cream or sherbets. There are manually-operated churns and several different models of electric ice cream makers that are better value, from those that work in the freezer to those that sit on the kitchen work surface and churn the mixture in a previously chilled container. Additionally, there are more expensive elec-

tric ice cream makers that are freestanding and have their own built-in freezing unit.

NUTMEG GRATER
Nutmeg should be used freshly ground and, as it is popular in Italian cooking, a nutmeg grater is to be found in every Italian kitchen.

MEZZALUNA
This semicircular knife is designed to rock backward and forward and is used for chopping ingredients such as herbs and nuts finely. It is often sold with a wooden board that has a dip in it. However, with the popularity of food processors its use has declined but you may find it useful for chopping small quantities and you have more control over the exact thickness of the food that you are chopping.

PARMESAN KNIFE
As mature Parmesan cheese is hard, Parmesan knives are designed not to cut, but to break off smaller pieces of cheese from a large piece and for scraping off slivers or slices.

PARMESAN GRATER
A special Parmesan grater is small and made of metal, so that you can grate the hard Parmesan cheese to exactly the right fineness required for sprinkling over a dish. A PARMESAN SHAVER, also made of metal, is used to shave the cheese.

PASTA MACHINE
These are convenient if you make a lot of pasta. A manual pasta machine rolls out and cuts the pasta dough into the size and shape that you require, such as sheets of lasagna or strips of tagliatelle. You can buy

extra attachments for some machines for making spaghetti and ravioli, and pasta-making attachments can be bought for some freestanding food mixers, which make different shapes such as spaghetti and macaroni. Electric pasta machines also mix the dough as well as rolling and cutting it but these machines are expensive and might be regarded as taking the enjoyment out of making pasta dough.

PASTA SCOOP

This strainer is ideal for scooping up long pasta such as spaghetti and comes in several designs. Some are metal spoons with a deep bowl, a slot in the base, and prongs around the edge and others are wooden spoons with prongs attached, sometimes called SPAGHETTI HOOKS.

PASTRY WHEEL

This is a small tool for cutting out pasta which, unlike a knife, does not drag the dough and gives a neat edge. It is particularly good for cutting out stuffed pasta such as ravioli.

PESTLE AND MORTAR

Often made of marble, these are used for crushing garlic and grinding peppercorns and spices. Choose a deep mortar with a rough inner surface to help with grinding.

PIZZA PAN

Made of metal with a perforated base, this is used for cooking a pizza in the oven so that the base remains crisp. A PIZZA STONE is preheated in the oven before the pizza is placed on it to cook. It absorbs moisture and helps produce the results of a professional pizza oven.

PIZZA WHEEL

This tool has a sharp circular blade which is used for slicing pizza without tearing it.

POLENTA EQUIPMENT

When polenta is cooked, it splutters and spits a lot and must be stirred constantly. A wooden spoon with a long handle is therefore essential to prevent it from burning you. If you make a lot of polenta, a PAIOLO, a copper pot with deep sides, is useful. A preserving pan or a large, deep, heavy-bottom pan are good alternatives.

RAVIOLI EQUIPMENT

A RAVIOLI CUTTER is a small tool with a wooden handle that has a square or round metal cutter attached. It is used to cut out individual pieces of ravioli. A RAVIOLI ROLLING PIN is a wooden pin with indentations in it that shape the squares of ravioli as you roll it over the dough and a RAVIOLI TRAY or GRID is a metal tray made up of about 36 squares over which the rolled out dough is placed, after which the squares are filled, a second piece of dough is placed on top, and, finally, a rolling pin is rolled over the top to make individual squares.

ROLLING PIN

A long, heavy wooden rolling pin is essential for rolling out pasta thinly. Italian rolling pins are at least 28 in/70 cm long.

SALAD DRAINER

This may come in the form of a wire basket with a handle, which is shaken, or a plastic container with a basket that fits inside, which is spun by pulling a string or turning a knob on the lid. Both are excellent for drying washed salad leaves thoroughly.

makes 1 quantity

basic pizza dough

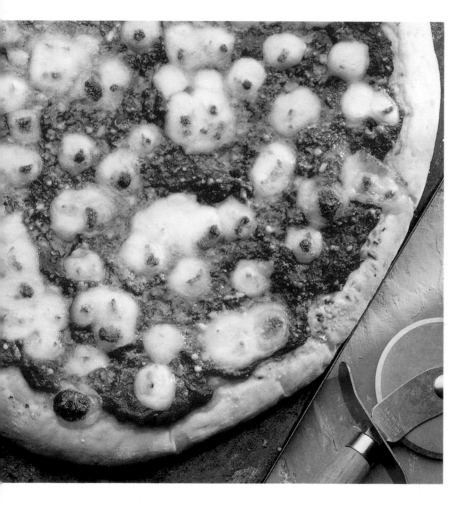

INGREDIENTS
½ oz/15 g dried yeast
1 tsp sugar
9 fl oz/250 ml hand-hot water
12 oz/350 g white bread flour
1 tsp salt
1 tsp olive oil

1 Put the yeast and sugar in a measuring cup and mix with 2 fl oz/50 ml of the water. Leave the mixture in a warm place for 15 minutes or until frothy.

2 In a large bowl, mix the flour with the salt and make a well in the center. Add the oil, the yeast mixture, and the remaining water. Using a wooden spoon, mix together to form a smooth dough.

3 Turn the dough out onto a floured counter and knead for 4–5 minutes until smooth.

4 Return the dough to the bowl, cover with a clean, damp dish towel, and let rise in a warm place for 30 minutes or until the dough has doubled in size.

5 Knead the dough for 2 minutes then stretch the dough with your hands to form a round. Place it on an oiled baking sheet, pushing out the edges until even. The dough should be no more than ¼ in/6 mm thick because it will rise during cooking.

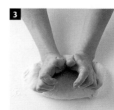

makes 1 quantity

basic pasta dough

INGREDIENTS
10 oz/280 g white bread flour, preferably
  «00» grade, plus extra for dusting
1 tsp salt
1 tbsp olive oil
2 eggs, beaten lightly

1 Lightly dust a counter with flour.
Sift the flour and salt into a mound
onto the counter.

2 Make a well in the center of the flour,
add the oil and beaten eggs, and, using
your fingertips, work to form a stiff dough.
If necessary, add 2–3 tablespoons water to
make the dough pliable.

3 Knead the dough vigorously for 8–10
minutes until the dough is smooth, firm and
soft. Wrap the dough in a plastic bag or
plastic wrap and let rest in the refrigerator
for 30 minutes.

4 Divide the dough into 2 equal pieces.
Cover a counter with a clean cloth or dish
towel and dust it liberally with flour. Place
one portion of the dough on the floured
cloth and roll it out as thinly and evenly as
possible, stretching the dough gently until
the pattern of the weave shows through.
Cover the rolled dough with a cloth while
rolling out the second piece. Alternatively,
use a pasta machine to cut the dough.

5 Using a ruler and a sharp-bladed knife,
or a pasta or pastry wheel, cut the pasta
into the required shapes, such as lasagna or
tagliatelle, or use a pasta machine to form
the dough into shapes.

6 To dry the pasta, place a dish towel over
the back of a chair and hang the strips over
it for 30–45 minutes to become partly dry.

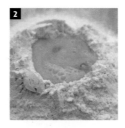
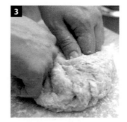

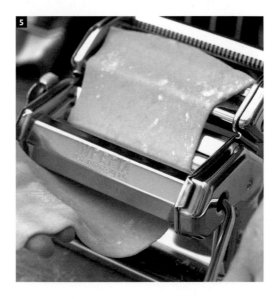

makes 1¼ cups

basic tomato sauce

INGREDIENTS
2 tbsp olive oil
1 small onion, chopped
1 garlic clove, chopped
14 oz/400 g canned chopped tomatoes
2 tbsp chopped fresh parsley
1 tsp dried oregano
2 bay leaves
2 tbsp tomato paste
1 tsp sugar
salt and pepper

1 Heat the oil in a pan over medium heat, add the onion, and fry for 2–3 minutes or until translucent. Add the garlic and fry for 1 minute.

2 Stir in the tomatoes, parsley, oregano, bay leaves, tomato paste, sugar, and salt and pepper to taste.

3 Bring the sauce to a boil, then simmer, uncovered, for 15–20 minutes or until the sauce has reduced by half. Taste the sauce and adjust the seasoning if necessary. Discard the bay leaves just before serving. This sauce keeps well in a screw-top jar in the refrigerator for up to 1 week.

makes 1¼ cups

béchamel sauce

INGREDIENTS
½ pint/300 ml milk
2 bay leaves
3 cloves
1 small onion
2 oz/55 g butter, plus extra for greasing
1½ oz/40 g all-purpose flour
½ pint/300 ml light cream
large pinch of freshly grated nutmeg
salt and pepper

1 Pour the milk into a small pan and add the bay leaves. Press the cloves into the onion, add to the pan, and bring the milk to a boil. Remove the pan from the heat and set aside to cool.

2 Strain the milk into a pitcher and rinse the pan. Melt the butter in the pan, stir in the flour, and cook for 1 minute, stirring. Remove from the heat and gradually pour in the milk, stirring constantly. Cook the sauce for 3 minutes, stirring, then pour in the cream and bring it to a boil. Remove from the heat and season with nutmeg, salt, and pepper to taste.

makes ½ cup

green pesto sauce

INGREDIENTS
40 fresh basil leaves
3 garlic cloves, crushed
1 oz/25 g pine nuts
1¾ oz/50 g Parmesan cheese, grated finely
2–3 tbsp extra virgin olive oil
salt and pepper

1 Rinse the basil leaves and pat them dry with kitchen paper. Put the basil leaves, garlic, pine nuts, and Parmesan into a food processor and blend for 30 seconds or until smooth. Alternatively, pound all of the ingredients in a mortar with a pestle.

2 If you are using a food processor, keep the motor running and slowly add the olive oil. Alternatively, add the oil drop by drop while stirring briskly. Season with salt and pepper to taste.

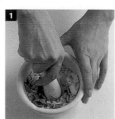

makes 3½ **pints/2 liters**

chicken stock

INGREDIENTS
2 lb 4 oz/1 kg chicken, skinned
2 celery sticks
1 large onion
2 carrots
1 garlic clove
fresh parsley sprigs
3½ pints/2 liters water
salt and pepper

1 Put all the ingredients into a large pan and bring to a boil over medium heat.

2 Using a slotted spoon skim any scum from the surface. Reduce the heat to a gentle simmer, partially cover, and cook for 2 hours, then let cool.

3 Line a strainer with clean cheesecloth and place over a large pitcher or bowl. Pour the stock through the strainer. The cooked chicken can be used in another recipe. Discard the other solids. Cover the stock and chill in the refrigerator.

4 Store in the refrigerator for 3–4 days until required, or freeze in small batches. Before using, skim off any fat that has formed.

makes 3½ **pints/2 liters**

vegetable stock

INGREDIENTS
9 oz/250 g shallots
1 large carrot, diced
1 celery stick, chopped
½ fennel bulb
1 garlic clove
1 bay leaf
fresh parsley sprigs
fresh tarragon sprigs
3½ pints/2 liters water
pepper

1 Put all the ingredients into a large pan and bring to a boil over medium heat.

2 Using a slotted spoon skim any scum from the surface. Reduce the heat to a gentle simmer, partially cover, and cook for 45 minutes, then let cool.

3 Line a strainer with clean cheesecloth and place over a large pitcher or bowl. Pour the stock through the strainer. Discard the herbs and vegetables.

4 Cover and store in small quantities in the refrigerator for up to 3 days. The stock can also be frozen in small quantities.

part one

ANTIPASTI
appetizers, soups & salads

There is a variety of antipasti to suit all tastes in this section. Choose just a few, a whole selection, or even serve the more substantial dishes as a light meal if preferred.

Soups are ideal for serving as a light beginning to a meal or as a meal in themselves, and the same applies to the salad recipes that follow. You are spoilt for choice!

serves 4 | prep 10 mins | cook 45 mins

crostini alla fiorentina

Serve as part of an antipasto, or spread on small pieces of crusty fried bread (crostini) as an appetizer with drinks.

INGREDIENTS
3 tbsp olive oil
1 onion, chopped
1 celery stalk, chopped
1 carrot, chopped
1–2 garlic cloves, crushed
4½ oz/125 g chicken livers
4½ oz/125 g calf's, lamb's, or pig's liver
⅔ cup red wine
1 tbsp tomato paste
2 tbsp chopped fresh parsley
3–4 canned anchovy fillets, chopped finely
2 tbsp stock or water
2–3 tbsp butter
1 tbsp capers
salt and pepper
small pieces of fried crusty bread, to serve
chopped parsley, to garnish

Heat the oil in a pan, add the onion, celery, carrot, and garlic, and cook gently for 4–5 minutes or until the onion has become soft, but not colored.

Meanwhile, rinse and dry the chicken livers. Dry the calf's liver, and slice into strips. Add the liver to the pan and fry gently for a few minutes until the strips are well sealed on all sides.

Add half of the wine and cook until it has mostly evaporated. Then add the rest of the wine, tomato paste, half of the parsley, the anchovy fillets, stock or water, a little salt, and plenty of black pepper.

Cover the pan and leave to simmer, stirring occasionally, for 15–20 minutes or until the liver is tender and most of the liquid has been absorbed.

Leave the mixture to cool a little, then either mince coarsely or put into a food processor and process to a chunky purée.

Return to the pan and add the butter, capers and remaining parsley. Heat through gently until the butter melts. Adjust the seasoning and turn out into a bowl. Serve warm or cold spread on the slices of crusty bread and sprinkled with chopped parsley.

serves 4 | prep 10 mins | cook 50 mins

leek & tomato timbales

Angel-hair pasta, known as cappellini, is mixed with fried leeks, sun-dried tomatoes, fresh oregano, and beaten eggs, and baked in ramekins.

INGREDIENTS
3 oz/90 g angel-hair pasta (cappellini)
2 tbsp butter
1 tbsp olive oil
1 large leek, sliced finely
½ cup sun-dried tomatoes in oil,
  drained and chopped
1 tbsp chopped fresh oregano
  or 1 tsp dried oregano
2 eggs, beaten
generous ⅓ cup light cream
1 tbsp freshly grated Parmesan
salt and pepper
sprigs of oregano, to garnish
lettuce leaves, to serve

for the tomato sauce
1 small onion, chopped finely
1 small garlic clove, crushed
12 oz/350 g tomatoes, peeled (see Cook's
  Tip on page 111) and chopped
1 tsp mixed dried Italian herbs
4 tbsp dry white wine

Cook the pasta in plenty of boiling salted water for about 3 minutes until «al dente» (just tender). Drain and rinse with cold water to cool quickly.

Meanwhile, heat the butter and oil in a skillet. Gently fry the leek until softened, about 5–6 minutes. Add the sun-dried tomatoes and oregano, and cook for a further 2 minutes. Remove from the heat.

Add the leek mixture to the pasta. Stir in the beaten eggs, cream, and Parmesan. Season with salt and pepper. Divide between 4 greased ramekin dishes or dariole molds.

Place the dishes in a roasting pan with enough warm water to come halfway up their sides. Bake in a preheated oven, 350°F/180°C, for about 30 minutes, until the mixture has set.

Meanwhile, make the tomato sauce. Fry the onion and garlic in the remaining butter and oil until softened. Add the tomatoes, herbs, and wine. Cover and cook gently for about 20 minutes until pulpy. Blend in a food processor until smooth, or press through a strainer.

Run a knife or small spatula around the edge of the ramekins, then turn out the timbales onto 4 warm serving plates. Pour over a little sauce and garnish with oregano. Serve with the lettuce leaves.

serves 4 | prep 10 mins | cook 25 mins

tuna-stuffed tomatoes

Deliciously sweet roasted tomatoes are filled with homemade lemon mayonnaise and tuna.

INGREDIENTS
4 plum tomatoes
2 tbsp sun-dried tomato paste
2 egg yolks
2 tsp lemon juice
finely grated rind of 1 lemon
4 tbsp olive oil
4 oz/115g canned tuna, drained
2 tbsp capers, rinsed
salt and pepper

to garnish
2 sun-dried tomatoes, cut into strips
fresh basil leaves

Halve the tomatoes and scoop out the seeds. Divide the sun-dried tomato paste among the tomato halves and spread around the inside of the skin.

Place on a cookie sheet and roast in a preheated oven at 400°F/200°C for 12–15 minutes. Leave to cool slightly.

Meanwhile, make the mayonnaise. In a food processor, blend the egg yolks and lemon juice with the lemon rind until smooth. Once mixed and with the motor still running slowly, add the olive oil. Stop the processor as soon as the mayonnaise has thickened. Alternatively, use a hand whisk, beating the mixture continuously until it thickens.

Add the tuna and capers to the mayonnaise and season.

Spoon the tuna mayonnaise mixture into the tomato shells and garnish with sun-dried tomato strips and basil leaves. Return to the oven for a few minutes or serve chilled.

COOKS TIP
For a picnic, do not roast the tomatoes, just scoop out the seeds, drain, cut-side down on absorbent paper towels for 1 hour, and fill with the mayonnaise mixture. They are firmer and easier to handle this way. If you prefer, shop-bought mayonnaise may be used instead—just stir in the lemon rind.

serves 4 | prep 10 mins | cook 8 mins

avocado margherita

Heat the olive oil in a skillet. Add the onion and garlic and fry gently for 2 minutes or until soft.

Peel the tomatoes using the method described in the Cook's Tip on page 111.

Arrange the avocado halves on a plate with the narrow ends pointed toward the center. Spoon the onion mixture into the hollow of each half.

Cut and slice the tomatoes in half. Divide the tomatoes, basil, and thin slices of mozzarella between the avocado halves. Season with salt and pepper to taste.

Place the avocado halves under a preheated medium broiler for 5–6 minutes or until the avocados are heated through and the cheese has melted. Transfer the avocados to serving plates, garnish with basil leaves, and serve with mixed salad leaves.

VARIATION
If you are using a combination microwave oven with broiler, arrange the avocados on the low rack of the broiler, or on the glass turntable. Cook on combination broiler 1 and LOW power for 8 minutes until the tops are browned and bubbling.

The colors of the tomatoes, basil, and mozzarella cheese in this patriotic recipe represent the colors of the Italian flag.

INGREDIENTS
1 small red onion, sliced
1 garlic clove, crushed
1 tbsp olive oil
2 small tomatoes
2 avocados, halved and stoned
4 fresh basil leaves, torn into shreds
2 oz/60 g mozzarella cheese, sliced thinly
salt and pepper
fresh basil leaves, to garnish
mixed salad leaves, to serve

serves 4 | prep 10 mins | cook 10 mins

tomato & mozzarella bruschetta

These simple toasts are filled with color and flavor. They are delicious as a speedy appetizer or as a light meal or snack.

INGREDIENTS
4 English muffins
4 garlic cloves, crushed
2 tbsp butter
1 tbsp chopped basil
4 large, ripe tomatoes, peeled
  (see Cook's Tip on page 111)
1 tbsp tomato paste
8 pitted black olives, halved
1¾ oz/50 g mozzarella cheese, sliced
salt and pepper
fresh basil leaves, to garnish

dressing
1 tbsp olive oil
2 tsp lemon juice
1 tsp clear honey

Cut the muffins in half to give eight thick pieces. Toast the muffin halves under a hot broiler for 2–3 minutes until golden.

Mix the garlic, butter, and basil together and spread onto each muffin half.

Chop the tomato flesh and mix with the tomato paste and olives. Divide the mixture between the muffins.

Mix the dressing ingredients and drizzle over each muffin.

Place a slice of mozzarella cheese on top of each muffin and season.

Return the muffins to the broiler for 1–2 minutes until the cheese melts.

Garnish with fresh basil leaves and serve at once.

VARIATION
Use balsamic vinegar instead of the lemon juice for a deliciously authentic Italian flavor.

serves 4 | prep 5 mins | cook 40 mins

fried risotto balls

The Italian name for this dish translates as «telephone wires,» which refers to the strings of melted mozzarella cheese contained within the risotto balls.

INGREDIENTS
2 tbsp olive oil
1 medium onion, chopped finely
1 garlic clove, chopped
½ red bell pepper, diced
¾ cup risotto rice, washed
1 tsp dried oregano
1⅔ cups hot Vegetable or Chicken Stock
  (see page 29)
scant ½ cup dry white wine
2¾ oz/75 g mozzarella cheese
oil, for frying
fresh basil sprig, to garnish

Heat the oil in a skillet and cook the onion and garlic for 3–4 minutes or until just softened.

Add the bell pepper, rice, and oregano to the skillet. Cook for 2–3 minutes, stirring to coat the rice in the oil.

Mix the stock together with the wine and add to the skillet a ladleful at a time, waiting for the liquid to be absorbed by the rice before you add the next ladleful of liquid.

Once all of the liquid has been absorbed and the rice is tender (it should take about 15 minutes in total), remove the skillet from the heat and leave until the mixture is cool enough to handle.

Cut the cheese into 12 pieces. Taking about 1 tablespoon of risotto, shape the mixture around the cheese pieces to make 12 balls.

Heat the oil until a cube of bread browns in 30 seconds. Cook the risotto balls, in batches of 4, for 2 minutes or until golden.

Remove the risotto balls with a slotted spoon and drain thoroughly on absorbent kitchen paper. Garnish with a sprig of basil and serve the risotto balls hot.

VARIATION
For an even cheesier flavor, stir in a tablespoon of grated Parmesan cheese before taking the risotto off the heat.

serves 4 | prep 20 mins | cook 30 mins

pancetta & pecorino cakes

These cakes also make an excellent light meal when served with a topping of pesto or anchovy sauce.

INGREDIENTS
2 tbsp butter, plus extra for greasing
3½ oz/100 g pancetta, rind removed
2 cups self-rising flour
⅞ cup grated pecorino cheese
⅝ cup milk, plus extra for glazing
1 tbsp tomato ketchup
1 tsp Worcestershire sauce
3½ cups dried farfalle
1 tbsp olive oil
salt and pepper
3 tbsp Green Pesto Sauce (see page 28)
  or anchovy sauce (optional)
green salad, to serve

Grease a cookie sheet with butter. Broil the pancetta until it is cooked. Allow the pancetta to cool, then chop finely.

Sift together the flour and a pinch of salt into a mixing bowl. Add the butter and rub in with your fingertips. When the butter and flour have been thoroughly incorporated, add the pancetta and one-third of the grated cheese.

Mix together the milk, tomato ketchup, and Worcestershire sauce and add to the dry ingredients, mixing to make a soft dough. Roll out the dough on a lightly floured board to make a 7-inch/18-cm round. Brush with a little milk to glaze and cut into 8 wedges.

Arrange the dough wedges on the prepared cookie sheet and sprinkle over the remaining cheese. Bake in a preheated oven at 400°F/200°C for 20 minutes.

Meanwhile, bring a pan of lightly salted water to a boil. Add the farfalle and the oil and cook for 8–10 minutes until just tender, but still firm to the bite. Drain and transfer to a large serving dish. Top with the pancetta and pecorino cakes. Serve with the sauce of your choice and a green salad.

serves 4 | prep 10 mins + 20 mins chilling | cook 0 mins

prosciutto with figs

This classic Italian appetizer couldn't be easier or more delicious. Paper-thin prosciutto di Parma has a uniquely aromatic flavor. Succulent fresh figs make a natural partnership.

INGREDIENTS
6 oz/175 g prosciutto di Parma,
  sliced thinly
pepper
4 fresh figs
1 lime
2 fresh basil sprigs

Using a sharp knife, trim the visible fat from the slices of ham and discard. Arrange the ham on 4 large serving plates, loosely folding it so that it falls into decorative shapes. Season to taste with pepper.

Using a sharp knife, cut each fig lengthwise into 4 wedges. Arrange a fig on each serving plate. Cut the lime into 6 wedges, place a wedge on each plate, and reserve the others. Remove the leaves from the basil sprigs and divide between the plates. Cover with plastic wrap and leave in the refrigerator to chill until ready to serve.

Just before serving, remove from the refrigerator and squeeze the juice from the remaining lime wedges over the prosciutto.

VARIATION
This dish is also delicious made with 4 slices of Charentais melon or 12–16 cooked and cooled asparagus spears, instead of the figs.

makes 16–30 | prep 10 mins | cook 20 mins

zucchini fritters

These tasty little fritters are a good one-dish antipasto and are great served as finger food at a drinks party.

INGREDIENTS
3½ oz/100 g self-rising flour
2 eggs, beaten
2 fl oz/50 ml milk
10½ oz/300 g zucchinis
2 tbsp fresh thyme
1 tbsp oil
salt and pepper

Sift the flour into a large bowl and make a well in the center. Add the eggs to the well and, using a wooden spoon, gradually draw in the flour.

Slowly add the milk to the mixture, stirring constantly to form a thick batter.

Meanwhile, wash the zucchinis. Grate them over a sheet of paper towel placed in a bowl to absorb some of the juices.

Add the zucchinis, thyme, and salt and pepper to taste to the batter and mix together thoroughly.

Heat the oil in a large, heavy-bottom skillet. Taking a tablespoon of the batter for a medium-size fritter or half a tablespoon of batter for a smaller fritter, spoon the mixture into the hot oil and cook, in batches, for 3–4 minutes on each side.

Remove the fritters with a slotted spoon and drain thoroughly on absorbent paper towels. Keep each batch of fritters warm in the oven while making the rest. Transfer to serving plates and serve hot.

VARIATION
Try adding ½ teaspoon of dried, crushed chilies to the batter with the thyme for spicier fritters.

serves 4 | prep 5 mins + 15 mins marinating | cook 0 mins

marinated raw beef

You need extremely thin slices of meat for this recipe. If you place the beef in the freezer for about 30 minutes, you will find it easier to slice.

INGREDIENTS
7 oz/200 g fillet of beef, in 1 piece
2 tbsp lemon juice
salt and pepper
4 tbsp extra virgin olive oil
2 oz/55 g Parmesan cheese, shaved thinly
4 tbsp chopped fresh flat-leaf parsley
lemon slices, to garnish
ciabatta or focaccia, to serve

VARIATION
To make Carpaccio di Tonno, substitute fresh, uncooked tuna for the fillet of beef. Do not use thawed frozen fish, and eat on the day of purchase.

Using a very sharp knife, cut the beef fillet into wafer-thin slices and arrange on 4 individual serving plates.

Pour the lemon juice into a small bowl and season to taste with salt and pepper. Beat in the olive oil, then pour the dressing over the meat. Cover the plates with plastic wrap and set aside for 10–15 minutes to marinate.

Remove and discard the plastic wrap. Arrange the Parmesan shavings in the center of each serving and sprinkle with parsley. Garnish with lemon slices and serve with fresh bread.

serves 4 | prep 5 mins | cook 0 mins

prosciutto with arugula

Arugula has become a fashionable salad vegetable in many homes and restaurants, but it has never been out of favor in Italy, where it grows wild.

INGREDIENTS
4 oz/115 g arugula
1 tbsp lemon juice
salt and pepper
3 tbsp extra virgin olive oil
8 oz/225 g prosciutto di Parma, sliced thinly

Separate the arugula leaves, wash in cold water, and pat dry on paper towels. Place the leaves in a bowl.

Pour the lemon juice into a small bowl and season to taste with salt and pepper. Beat in the olive oil, then pour the dressing over the arugula leaves and toss lightly so they are evenly coated.

Carefully drape the prosciutto in folds on 4 individual serving plates, then add the arugula. Serve at room temperature.

VARIATION
For a more substantial salad, add 1 thinly sliced fennel bulb and 2 thinly sliced oranges to the arugula in step 1. Substitute orange juice or balsamic vinegar for the lemon juice in step 2.

serves 4 | prep 10 mins | cook 0 mins

italian platter

This popular hors d'oeuvre usually consists of vegetables soaked in olive oil and rich, creamy cheeses. Try this great lowfat version as a guilt-free appetizer.

INGREDIENTS
4½ oz/125 g reduced-fat mozzarella cheese, drained
2 oz/60 g lean prosciutto di Parma
14 oz/400 g canned artichoke hearts, drained
4 ripe figs
1 small mango
few plain bread sticks, to serve

for the dressing
1 small orange
1 tbsp sieved tomatoes
1 tsp wholegrain mustard
4 tbsp lowfat plain yogurt
fresh basil leaves
salt and pepper

Cut the cheese into 12 sticks, 2½ inches/6.5 cm long. Remove the fat from the ham and slice the meat into 12 strips. Carefully wrap a strip of ham around each stick of cheese and arrange neatly on a serving platter.

Halve the artichoke hearts, cut the figs into fourths, and arrange them on the platter.

Peel the mango, then slice it down each side of the large, flat central stone. Slice the flesh into strips and arrange them to form a fan shape on the serving platter.

To make the dressing, pare the rind from half of the orange using a vegetable peeler.

Cut the rind into small strips and place them in a bowl. Extract the juice from the orange and add it to the bowl containing the rind.

Add the sieved tomatoes, mustard, yogurt, and seasoning to the bowl and mix together. Shred the basil leaves into small pieces and mix them into the dressing.

Spoon the dressing into a small dish and serve with the Italian Platter, accompanied with bread sticks.

serves 6 | prep 15 mins | cook 0 mins

antipasto volente

In Italy, antipasti are served as appetizers before the pasta course. The name of this dish translates as «take your pick.»

INGREDIENTS
7 oz/200 g canned tuna in oil, drained and
  flaked into chunks
4 oz/115 g canned sardines in
  oil, drained
3½ oz/100 g canned anchovy fillets
  in oil, drained
6 oz/175 g cooked shelled
  shrimp, deveined
4 oz/115 g prosciutto, cut into strips
6 oz/175 g mozzarella cheese, sliced
13½ oz/390 g canned artichoke hearts,
  drained and halved lengthwise
3 fresh figs, sliced
8 oz/225 g canned asparagus
  spears, drained
4 oz/115 g smoked salmon, sliced thinly
salt and pepper
⅔ cup black olives
extra virgin olive oil, for drizzling
lemon wedges, to garnish

Arrange the tuna, sardines, anchovies, shrimp, prosciutto, mozzarella cheese, artichoke hearts, and figs on a large serving platter.

Wrap 2–3 asparagus spears in each slice of smoked salmon and add to the platter. Season the antipasto to taste with salt and pepper.

Sprinkle the olives over the platter and drizzle with the olive oil. Garnish with lemon wedges, then serve immediately or cover with plastic wrap and let chill in the refrigerator until required, but bring to room temperature before serving.

VARIATION
If you like, use the same amount of fresh asparagus spears, instead of canned. Steam or cook in boiling water for 5 7 minutes, or until tender.

serves 4 | prep 20 mins | cook 1 hr

roman artichokes

The Roman contribution to this dish of stuffed artichokes is to flavor it with mint. Italian or Roman mint has a particularly sweet flavor, but you could use ordinary garden mint or one of the more exciting varieties, such as lemon or apple mint.

INGREDIENTS
5 tbsp lemon juice
4 globe artichokes
1 garlic clove
4 sprigs fresh flat-leaf parsley
2 sprigs fresh mint
1 lemon, cut into fourths
4 tbsp olive oil
salt and pepper
2 tbsp dry, uncolored bread crumbs
2 garlic cloves, chopped finely
2 tbsp fresh flat-leaf parsley,
   chopped coarsely
2 tbsp fresh mint, chopped coarsely
1 tbsp unsalted butter, diced

Select a bowl large enough to accommodate the prepared artichokes and fill with cold water and 4 tablespoons of the lemon juice. Working on one artichoke at a time, snap off the stems, then peel away the tough outer leaves. Snip or break off the tough tops of the remaining leaves. When the central cone of the artichoke appears, cut off the top ¾ inch/2 cm with a sharp knife. Drop the prepared artichokes into the acidulated water to prevent them from discoloring.

Place the artichokes in a heavy-bottom pan that is large enough to hold them firmly upright in a single layer. Add the whole garlic clove, parsley sprigs, mint sprigs, lemon fourths, and olive oil, and season to taste with salt and pepper. Pour in enough water to come two-thirds of the way up the sides of the pan. Bring to a boil over low heat, cover tightly, and let simmer for about 15 minutes, until the artichokes are nearly tender.

Meanwhile, combine the bread crumbs, chopped garlic, parsley, and mint in a bowl, and season to taste with salt and pepper.

Remove the artichokes from the pan and set aside to cool slightly. When they are cold enough to handle, gently separate the leaves, remove the central bearded chokes or cones with a teaspoon and discard. Season the artichokes to taste with salt and pepper. Return them to the pan, again standing them upright in a single layer. Spoon the bread crumb mixture into the centers, cover tightly, and cook over low heat for 20–30 minutes, until tender.

Using a slotted spoon, transfer the artichokes to 4 individual serving plates and set aside. Strain the cooking liquid into a clean pan and bring to a boil over high heat. Cook until reduced by about one-quarter or until the juices are concentrated, then reduce the heat and stir in the remaining lemon juice. Add the butter, a piece at a time, swirling the sauce in the pan until the butter has melted. Do not let the sauce boil. When all the butter has been incorporated, remove the pan from the heat. Serve the artichokes still warm and hand round the sauce separately.

serves 6 | prep 45 mins | cook 2 hrs 15 mins

minestrone

There are as many variations of this classic Italian soup as there are Italian cooks. You can use almost any vegetable in season to make minestrone. You can also add a little chopped pancetta or lean bacon to the mix to give the soup a bit more body. *

INGREDIENTS
2 fresh basil sprigs
2 fresh marjoram sprigs
2 fresh thyme sprigs
2 tbsp olive oil
2 onions, chopped
2 garlic cloves, chopped
4 tomatoes, peeled (see Cook's Tip on page 111) and chopped
½ cup red wine
7 cups Vegetable Stock (see page 29)
⅔ cup Great Northern beans, soaked overnight in cold water, then drained
2 carrots, chopped
2 potatoes, chopped
1 small turnip, chopped
1 celery stalk, chopped
¼ small cabbage, shredded
2 oz/55 g dried soup pasta shapes
salt and pepper
2 tbsp freshly grated Parmesan cheese, plus extra for serving

Chop enough fresh basil, marjoram, and thyme to fill 2 tablespoons and reserve until required. Heat the olive oil in a heavy-bottom pan. Add the onions and cook, stirring occasionally, for 5 minutes, or until softened. Stir in the garlic and cook for an additional 3 minutes, then stir in the chopped tomatoes and the reserved herbs.

Add the wine, simmer for 1–2 minutes, then add the stock and drained beans. Bring to a boil, then reduce the heat, partially cover, and simmer for 1½ hours.

Add the carrots, potatoes, and turnip, then cover and simmer for 15 minutes. Add the celery, cabbage, and pasta, then cover and simmer for an additional 10 minutes. Season to taste with salt and pepper and stir in the Parmesan cheese. Ladle into warmed bowls and serve with extra Parmesan cheese.

COOK'S TIP
*If you are a meat-eater you can add 2 slices of pancetta, or Italian bacon, rinded and chopped, to the soup with the garlic. It is available from Italian delicatessens and adds an extra depth of flavor to the soup.

serves 4 | prep 10 mins | cook 25 mins

creamy tomato soup

Soup made from fresh tomatoes is nothing like canned or packaged soups and is destined to become a firm family favorite.

INGREDIENTS
2 oz/55 g butter
1 onion, chopped finely
1 lb 9 oz/700 g tomatoes,
    chopped finely
salt and pepper
2½ cups hot Chicken
    or Vegetable Stock (see page 29)
pinch of sugar
generous ⅓ cup light cream
2 tbsp shredded fresh basil leaves
1 tbsp chopped fresh parsley

Melt half the butter in a large, heavy-bottom pan. Add the onion and cook over low heat, stirring occasionally, for 5 minutes, or until softened. Add the tomatoes, season to taste with salt and pepper, and cook for 5 minutes.

Pour in the hot stock, return to a boil, then reduce the heat, and cook for 10 minutes.

Push the soup through a strainer with the back of a wooden spoon to remove the tomato skins and seeds.

Return to the pan and stir in the sugar, cream, remaining butter, basil, and parsley. Heat through briefly, but do not let boil. Ladle the soup into warmed bowls and serve immediately.

VARIATION
Replace the chopped fresh parsley with the same amount of chopped fresh chives and serve with freshly grated Parmesan cheese sprinkled on the top.

serves 4 | prep 1 hr + 6 hrs chilling | cook 5 hrs

beef soup with eggs

Good-quality, homemade beef consommé is essential for this unusual soup. It is best to make it 24 hours in advance so that you can remove every trace of fat from the surface of the consommé.

INGREDIENTS
1 lb 2 oz/500 g beef marrow bones, sawn
   into 3-inch/7.5-cm pieces
12 oz/350 g stewing beef, in 1 piece
6 cups water
4 cloves
2 onions, halved
2 celery stalks, chopped coarsely
8 peppercorns
1 bouquet garni

2 oz/55 g unsalted butter
4 slices fresh white bread
1 cup freshly grated Parmesan cheese
4 eggs
salt and pepper

First, make the consommé. Place the bones in a large, heavy-bottom pan with the stewing beef on top. Add the water and bring to a boil over low heat, skimming off all the scum that rises to the surface. Pierce a clove into each onion half and add to the pan with the celery, peppercorns, and bouquet garni. Partially cover and let simmer very gently for 3 hours. Remove the meat and let simmer for an additional hour.

Strain the consommé into a bowl and set aside to cool. When completely cold, let chill in the refrigerator for at least 6 hours, preferably overnight. Carefully remove and discard the layer of fat that has formed on the surface. Return the consommé to a clean pan and heat until almost boiling.

When you are ready to serve, melt the butter in a heavy-bottom skillet. Add the bread, 1 slice at a time if necessary, and cook over medium heat until crisp and golden on both sides. Remove from the skillet and place one each in the base of 4 warmed soup bowls.

Sprinkle half the Parmesan over the fried bread. Carefully break an egg* over each slice of fried bread, keeping the yolks whole. Season to taste with salt and pepper and sprinkle with the remaining Parmesan. Carefully ladle the hot consommé into the soup bowls and serve immediately.

COOK'S TIP
*If you prefer, you could lightly poach the eggs before placing them on the fried bread slices.

serves 4 | prep 15 mins | cook 2 hrs 50 mins

white bean soup

Drain the soaked beans and place them in a large, heavy-bottom pan. Add the stock and bring to a boil. Partially cover the pan, reduce the heat, and let simmer for 2 hours, until tender.

Transfer about half the beans and a little of the stock to a food processor or blender and process to a smooth purée. Return the purée to the pan and stir well to mix. Bring the soup back to a boil.

Add the pasta to the soup, bring back to a boil and cook for 10 minutes, until tender.

Meanwhile, heat 4 tablespoons of the olive oil in a small pan. Add the garlic and cook over low heat, stirring frequently, for 4–5 minutes, until golden. Stir the garlic into the soup and add the parsley. Season to taste with salt and pepper and ladle into warmed soup bowls. Drizzle with the remaining olive oil and serve immediately.

VARIATION
Substitute cranberry beans for the cannellini beans and cook for about 1½ hours.

Beans feature widely in Tuscan cuisine. This smooth, comforting soup, in which beans are simmered for 2 hours, is very simple to make. Garlic and parsley, stirred in just before serving, complement the flavor, and a drizzle of olive oil adds the final touch.

INGREDIENTS
1 cup dried cannellini beans, covered and soaked overnight in cold water
7 cups Chicken or Vegetable Stock (see page 29)
4 oz/115 g soup pasta
6 tbsp olive oil
2 garlic cloves, chopped finely
4 tbsp chopped fresh flat-leaf parsley
salt and pepper

serves 4 | prep 5 mins | cook 3hrs 15 mins

veal & ham soup

Veal and ham is a classic combination, complemented here with the addition of cream sherry to create a richly-flavored Italian soup.

INGREDIENTS
4 tbsp butter
1 onion, diced
1 carrot, diced
1 celery stalk, diced
1 lb/450 g veal, sliced very thinly
1 lb/450 g ham, sliced thinly
½ cup all-purpose flour
4⅜ cups beef stock
1 bay leaf
8 black peppercorns
pinch of salt
3 tbsp red currant jelly
⅝ cup cream sherry
¾ cup dried vermicelli
garlic croûtons,* to serve

Melt the butter in a large pan. Add the onions, carrot, celery, veal, and ham and cook over low heat for 6 minutes.

Sprinkle over the flour and cook, stirring constantly, for a further 2 minutes. Gradually stir in the stock, then add the bay leaf, peppercorns, and salt. Bring to a boil and simmer for 1 hour.

Remove the pan from the heat and add the red currant jelly and cream sherry, stirring to combine. Set aside for about 4 hours.

Remove the bay leaf from the pan and discard. Reheat the soup over very low heat until warmed through.

Meanwhile, cook the vermicelli in a pan of lightly salted boiling water for 10–12 minutes. Stir the vermicelli into the soup and transfer to soup bowls. Serve with garlic croûtons.

COOK'S TIP
*To make garlic croutons, remove the crusts from 3 slices of day-old white bread. Cut the bread into ¼-inch/5-mm cubes. Heat 3 tablespoons oil over low heat and stir-fry 1–2 chopped garlic cloves for 1–2 minutes. Remove the garlic and add the bread. Cook, stirring frequently, until golden. Remove with a slotted spoon and drain.

serves 4 | prep 20 mins | cook 35 mins

seafood soup

Full of delicious Mediterranean flavors, this soup is both less heavy and much easier to make than its French Provençal cousin bouillabaisse.

INGREDIENTS
4 tbsp olive oil
1 garlic clove, sliced
2 tbsp chopped fresh flat-leaf parsley
1 dried red chili, whole
7 oz/200 g canned plum tomatoes, chopped
1 cod or haddock head
½ cup dry white wine
3½ cups boiling water
salt
1 lb/450 g angler fish fillet
10 oz/280 g live mussels
1 lb/450 g uncooked shrimp
salt and pepper
4 slices sfilatino or French bread,
   each ¾ inch/2 cm thick

Heat half the olive oil in a large, heavy-bottom pan. Add the garlic, half the parsley, and the chili and cook over low heat, stirring occasionally, for 3 minutes, until the garlic starts to color. Add the tomatoes, fish head, and wine and continue to cook until almost all the liquid has gone. Add the boiling water, season with salt, and let simmer for 20 minutes.

Meanwhile, remove the gray membrane from the angler fish and cut the flesh into bite-size pieces. Scrub the mussels under cold running water and tug off the beards. Discard any mussels with broken or damaged shells and those that do not shut immediately when sharply tapped. Shell the shrimp, cut a slit along the back of each, and remove and discard the dark vein.

Add the angler fish and mussels to the pan and let simmer for 4–5 minutes. Add the shrimp and let simmer for an additional 2–3 minutes, until they have changed color.

Remove and discard the fish head and the chili. Remove any mussels that have not opened. Add the remaining olive oil and parsley to the soup, taste, and adjust the seasoning if necessary.

Toast the bread and put a slice in the base of 4 warmed soup bowls. Ladle the soup over the bread and serve immediately.

serves 4 | prep 2 mins | cook 10 mins

tuscan bean soup

A thick and creamy soup that is based on a traditional Tuscan recipe. If you use dried beans, the preparation and cooking times will be longer.

INGREDIENTS
8 oz/225 g dried lima beans, soaked overnight, or 2 x 14 oz/400 g canned lima beans
1 tbsp olive oil
2 garlic cloves, crushed
1 vegetable or chicken stock cube, crumbled
⅔ cup milk
2 tbsp chopped fresh oregano
salt and pepper

If you are using dried beans that have been soaked overnight, drain them thoroughly. Bring a large pan of water to a boil, add the beans, and boil for 10 minutes. Cover the pan and simmer for a further 30 minutes or until tender. Drain the beans, reserving the cooking liquid. If you are using canned beans, drain them thoroughly and reserve the liquid.

Heat the oil in a large skillet and fry the garlic for 2–3 minutes or until just beginning to brown.

Add the beans and 1⅔ cup of the reserved liquid to the skillet, stirring constantly. You may need to add a little water if there is insufficient liquid. Stir in the crumbled stock cube. Bring the mixture to a boil, stirring, and then remove the skillet from the heat.

Place the bean mixture in a food processor and blend to form a smooth paste. Alternatively, mash the bean mixture to a smooth consistency. Season to taste with salt and pepper and stir in the milk.

Pour the soup back into the skillet and gently heat to just below boiling point. Stir in the chopped oregano just before serving.

serves 8 | prep 15 mins | cook 1 hr 45 mins

genoese vegetable soup

*This classic vegetable soup is served
with an equally classic pesto sauce that
originated in the Ligurian port of Genoa.
It makes a wonderful dish for an informal
dinner with family and friends.*

INGREDIENTS
2 onions, sliced
2 carrots, diced
2 celery stalks, sliced
2 potatoes, diced
¾ cup green beans, cut into 1-inch/2.5-cm
    lengths
1 cup peas, thawed if using frozen
4½ cups fresh spinach leaves, coarse stalks
    removed, shredded
2 zucchinis, diced
8 oz/225 g Italian plum tomatoes, peeled
    (see Cook's Tip on page 111), seeded,
    and diced
3 garlic cloves, sliced thinly
4 tbsp extra virgin olive oil
8 cups Vegetable or Chicken Stock
    (see page 29)
salt and pepper
5 oz/140 g dried stellete or other soup pasta
freshly grated Parmesan cheese, to serve
1 quantity Green Pesto Sauce (see page 28)

Put the onions, carrots, celery, potatoes, beans, peas, spinach,
zucchinis, tomatoes, and garlic in a large, heavy-bottom pan,
pour in the olive oil and stock and bring to a boil over medium-low
heat. Reduce the heat and let simmer gently for about 1½ hours.

Season the soup to taste with salt and pepper and add the pasta.
Cook for an additional 8–10 minutes, until the pasta is tender, but
still firm to the bite. The soup should be very thick.

Stir in half the Green Pesto Sauce, remove the pan from the heat
and set aside to rest for 4 minutes. Taste and adjust the seasoning,
adding more salt, pepper, and Green Pesto Sauce if necessary.

Ladle into warmed bowls and serve immediately. Hand round the
freshly grated Parmesan cheese separately.

VARIATION
*Instead of soup pasta, add 5 oz/140 g
cooked long-grain rice just before the
end of the cooking time and continue
cooking the soup just long enough to
heat the rice through before setting the
soup aside to rest.*

serves 4 | prep 20 mins | cook 5 mins

capri salad

This tomato, olive, and mozzarella salad, dressed with balsamic vinegar and olive oil, makes a delicious antipasto.

INGREDIENTS
2 beefsteak tomatoes
4½ oz/125 g fresh mozzarella cheese, drained
12 black olives
8 basil leaves
1 tbsp balsamic vinegar
1 tbsp olive oil
salt and pepper
basil leaves, to garnish

Using a sharp knife, cut the tomatoes into thin slices.

Using a sharp knife, cut the mozzarella into slices.

Pit the olives and slice them into rings.

Layer the tomato, mozzarella cheese, and olives in a stack, finishing with a layer of cheese on top.

Place each stack under a preheated hot broiler for 2–3 minutes or just long enough to melt the mozzarella.

Drizzle over the vinegar and olive oil, and season to taste with a little salt and pepper.

Transfer to serving plates and garnish with basil leaves. Serve immediately.

serves 4 | prep 15 mins | cook 1 hr 45 mins

beans with tuna

This is a truly mouthwatering dish that has been horribly corrupted by cheap trattorie that are no more Italian than a sushi bar. Forget any ghastly memories of canned beans and tuna and try the real thing. For hungry people you might allow 1 tuna steak each, but the beans are very filling.

INGREDIENTS
1 lb 12 oz/800 g Great Northern beans,
   covered and soaked overnight in cold water
6 tbsp extra virgin olive oil
2 x 7 oz/200 g tuna steaks
2 garlic cloves, crushed lightly
sprig fresh sage
2 tbsp water
salt and pepper
4 chopped fresh sage leaves, to garnish

Drain the soaked beans and place them in a pan. Add enough water to cover and bring to a boil. Reduce the heat and let simmer for 1–1½ hours, until tender. Drain the beans thoroughly.

Heat 1 tablespoon of the olive oil in a heavy-bottom skillet. Add the tuna steaks and cook over medium heat for 3–4 minutes on each side, until tender. Remove from the skillet and set aside to cool.

Heat 3 tablespoons of the remaining olive oil in a heavy-bottom skillet. Add the garlic and sage sprig and cook briefly over low heat until the sage starts to sizzle. Remove the garlic and discard.

Add the beans and cook for 1 minute, then add the measured water and season to taste with salt and pepper. Cook until the water has been absorbed. Remove and discard the sage sprig, transfer the beans to a bowl, and set aside to cool.

Meanwhile, flake the tuna, removing any bones. When the beans are lukewarm or at room temperature, according to taste, gently stir in the tuna. Drizzle with the remaining olive oil, sprinkle with the chopped sage, and serve.

serves 4 | prep 15 mins | cook 0 mins

artichoke & arugula salad

This simple Tuscan salad is made from the small, tender artichokes of the early summer. The tart flavor of the lemons is perfectly complemented by the saltiness of the pecorino cheese.

INGREDIENTS
8 baby globe artichokes
juice of 2 lemons
bunch of arugula
salt and pepper
½ cup extra virgin olive oil
4 oz/115 g pecorino cheese

Break off the stems of the artichokes and cut off about 1 inch/2.5 cm of the tops, depending on how young and small they are. Remove and discard any coarse outer leaves, leaving only the pale, tender inner leaves. Using a teaspoon scoop out the chokes. Rub each artichoke with lemon juice as soon as it is prepared to prevent it from discoloring.

Thinly slice the artichokes and place in a salad bowl. Add the arugula, lemon juice, and olive oil, season to taste with salt and pepper, and toss well.

Using a swivel-blade vegetable peeler, thinly shave the pecorino over the salad, then serve immediately.

VARIATION
This salad can also be made from the artichoke's close relation, the cardoon. Cut off and discard the tough, outer stalks.

serves 4 | prep 15 mins + 8 hrs chilling | cook 0 mins

layered tomato salad

This is a popular salad throughout Italy and the perfect way of using up yesterday's bread. For the fullest flavor, use sun-ripened tomatoes.

INGREDIENTS
1 red onion, sliced thinly into rings
4 slices day-old bread
1 lb/450 g tomatoes, sliced thinly
4 oz/115 g fresh mozzarella cheese, drained
  and sliced thinly
1 tbsp shredded fresh basil
salt and pepper
½ cup extra virgin olive oil
3 tbsp balsamic vinegar
4 tbsp lemon juice
⅔ cup black olives, pitted and sliced thinly

VARIATION
To enhance the flavor of the tomatoes chop 1 oz/25 g sundried tomatoes over the salad before serving.

Place the onion slices in a bowl and add cold water to cover. Set aside to soak for 10 minutes. Meanwhile, dip the slices of bread in a shallow dish of cold water, then squeeze out the excess. Place the bread in a serving dish.

Drain the onion slices and layer them on the bread with the tomatoes and mozzarella, sprinkling each layer with the basil and salt and pepper.

Pour over the olive oil, vinegar, and lemon juice, and sprinkle with the sliced olives. Cover and let chill for up to 8 hours before serving.

serves 4 | prep 15 mins | cook 10 mins

goat cheese, pear & walnut salad

In this popular combination of ingredients the delicate flavor of the goat cheese combines beautifully with the sweet pears and slightly bitter walnuts.

INGREDIENTS
2¼ cups dried penne
1 head radicchio, torn into pieces
1 Webbs lettuce, torn into pieces
7 tbsp chopped walnuts
2 ripe pears, cored and diced
⅝ cup arugula, trimmed
2 tbsp lemon juice
5 tbsp olive oil
1 garlic clove, chopped
3 tbsp white wine vinegar
4 tomatoes, cut into fourths
1 small onion, sliced
1 large carrot, grated
9 oz/250 g goat cheese, diced
salt and pepper

Bring a large pan of lightly salted water to a boil over medium heat. Add the pasta and cook until done. Drain the pasta thoroughly and refresh in cold water, then drain again and set aside to cool.

Put the radicchio and Webbs lettuce into a large salad bowl and mix together well. Top with the cooled pasta, chopped walnuts, pears, and arugula.

Mix the lemon juice, oil, garlic, and vinegar together in a measuring cup. Pour the mixture over the salad ingredients and toss to coat the salad leaves well.

Add the tomato fourths, onion slices, grated carrot, and diced goat cheese and toss together with 2 forks, until well mixed. Let the salad chill in the refrigerator for about 1 hour before serving.

COOK'S TIP
Most goat cheese comes from France and there are many varieties, such as Crottin de Chavignol, Chabi, which is very pungent, and Sainte-Maure, which is available in creamery and farmhouse varieties.

serves 4 | prep 5 mins + 30 mins chilling | cook 0 mins

insalata tricolore

With the white mozzarella, red tomatoes, and green basil representing the colors of the Italian flag, this salad is served all over Italy and beyond.

INGREDIENTS
10 oz/280 g fresh mozzarella cheese, drained
   and sliced thinly
8 plum tomatoes, sliced
salt and pepper
20 fresh basil leaves
½ cup extra virgin olive oil

Arrange the cheese and tomato slices on 4 individual serving plates and season to taste with salt. Set aside in a cool place for 30 minutes.

Sprinkle the basil leaves over the salad and drizzle with the olive oil. Season with pepper and serve immediately.

VARIATION
There are dozens of variations of this popular and refreshing salad. Add 24 pitted black olives and 5 drained and chopped anchovies before adding the basil. Alternatively, peel, halve, and pit 2 avocados. Cut the flesh crosswise into thin slices and arrange them over the salad before sprinkling with the basil. Thinly slice a small white and a small red onion and push out into rings. Arrange them on top of the salad before sprinkling with the basil.

part two

PRIMI PIATTI
pasta & rice

Pasta and rice are served as a first course in the
Italian menu but there is no reason why you can't
serve them as a meal on their own, accompanied
by a salad. Many Italians eat these dishes every
day, so it is no wonder there are so many different
recipes to ring the changes.

serves 4 | prep 15 mins | cook 8–10 mins

pasta with pesto

Homemade pesto is much more delicious than even good-quality, store-bought brands and it makes a wonderful no-cook sauce for all types of freshly cooked pasta.

INGREDIENTS
1 lb/450 g dried spaghetti
fresh basil sprigs, to garnish (optional)
1 quantity Green Pesto Sauce
  (see page 28)

Bring a large heavy-bottom pan of lightly salted water to a boil. Add the pasta, return to a boil, and cook for 8–10 minutes, or until tender but still firm to the bite.

Drain the pasta and set aside 1–2 tablespoons of the cooking water.

If you like, thin the Green Pesto Sauce slightly with the cooking water, then add to the pasta and toss well. Serve immediately, garnished with basil, if you like.

COOK'S TIP
For a green pesto with a completely different flavor, replace the basil in the Green Pesto Sauce with a large bunch of arugula, about 3½ oz/100 g.

serves 4 | prep 10 mins | cook 8–10 mins

tagliatelle with walnuts

This unusual combination would make an intriguing appetizer for a dinner party, but is also great for a light lunch, if served with a crisp green salad and crusty bread.

INGREDIENTS
½ cup fresh white bread crumbs
3 cups walnut pieces
2 garlic cloves, chopped finely
4 tbsp milk
4 tbsp olive oil
⅜ cup cream cheese
⅔ cup light cream
salt and pepper
12 oz/350 g dried tagliatelle

Place the bread crumbs, walnuts, garlic, milk, olive oil, and cream cheese in a large mortar and grind to a smooth paste. Alternatively, place the ingredients in a food processor and process until smooth. Stir in the cream to give a thick sauce consistency and season to taste with salt and pepper. Set aside.

Bring a large heavy-bottom pan of lightly salted water to a boil. Add the pasta, return to a boil, and cook for 8–10 minutes, or until tender but still firm to the bite.

Drain the pasta and transfer to a warmed serving dish. Add the walnut sauce and toss thoroughly to coat. Serve immediately.

serves 4 | prep 5 mins | cook 15 mins

spaghetti olio & aglio

Cooked pasta gets cold quickly, so make sure that the serving dish is warmed thoroughly, and as soon as the pasta is drained, transfer to the dish.

INGREDIENTS
1 lb/450 g dried spaghetti
½ cup extra virgin olive oil
3 garlic cloves, finely chopped
3 tbsp chopped fresh
   flat-leaf parsley
salt and pepper

Bring a large, heavy-bottom pan of lightly salted water to a boil. Add the spaghetti, return to a boil, and cook for 8–10 minutes, or until tender but still firm to the bite.

Meanwhile, heat the olive oil in a heavy-bottom skillet. Add the garlic and a pinch of salt and cook over low heat, stirring constantly, for 3–4 minutes, or until golden. Do not allow the garlic to brown or it will taste bitter. Remove the skillet from the heat.

Drain the pasta and transfer to a warmed serving dish. Pour in the garlic-flavored olive oil, then add the chopped parsley and season to taste with salt and pepper. Toss well and serve immediately.

serves 6 | prep 15 mins | cook 45 mins

spaghetti with meatballs

Every Italian mamma has her own version of this dish, which, naturally, is the best.

INGREDIENTS
1 potato, diced
1¾ cups ground steak
1 onion, chopped finely
1 egg
4 tbsp chopped fresh flat-leaf parsley
all-purpose flour, for dusting
5 tbsp virgin olive oil
1¾ cups strained tomatoes
2 tbsp tomato paste
14 oz/400 g dried spaghetti
salt and pepper

to garnish
6 fresh basil leaves, shredded
freshly grated Parmesan cheese

Place the potato in a small pan, add cold water to cover and a pinch of salt, and bring to a boil. Cook for 10–15 minutes, until tender, then drain. Either cream thoroughly with a potato creamer or fork or pass through a potato ricer.

Combine the potato, steak, onion, egg, and parsley in a bowl and season to taste with salt and pepper. Spread out the flour on a plate. With dampened hands, shape the meat mixture into walnut-size balls and roll in the flour. Shake off any excess.

Heat the oil in a heavy-bottom skillet, add the meatballs, and cook over medium heat, stirring and turning frequently, for 8–10 minutes, until golden all over.

Add the strained tomatoes and tomato paste and cook for an additional 10 minutes, until the sauce is reduced and slightly thickened.

Meanwhile, bring a large pan of lightly salted water to a boil. Add the pasta, bring back to a boil, and cook for 8–10 minutes, until tender, but still firm to the bite.

Drain well and add to the meatball sauce, tossing well to coat. Transfer to a warmed serving dish, garnish with the basil leaves and Parmesan and serve immediately.

serves 4 | prep 20 mins | cook 40 mins

macaroni with roasted vegetables

Roasting Mediterranean vegetables brings out their sweetness and full flavor to make a naturally rich sauce for pasta.

INGREDIENTS
2 red onions, cut into wedges
2 zucchinis, cut into chunks
1 red bell pepper, seeded and
   cut into chunks
1 yellow bell pepper, seeded and
   cut into chunks
1 eggplant, cut into chunks
1 lb/450 g plum tomatoes,
   cut into fourths and seeded
3 garlic cloves, chopped
4 tbsp olive oil
salt and pepper
12 oz/350 g dried short-cut macaroni
1¼ cups strained tomatoes
½ cup black olives, pitted and halved

to garnish
fresh basil sprigs
fresh flat-leaf parsley sprigs

Preheat the oven to 475°F/240°C. Spread out the onions, zucchinis, bell peppers, eggplant, and tomatoes in a single layer in a large roasting pan. Sprinkle with the garlic, drizzle with the olive oil, and season to taste with salt and pepper. Stir well until all the vegetables are coated. Roast in the preheated oven for 15 minutes, then remove from the oven and stir well. Return to the oven for an additional 15 minutes.

Bring a large heavy-bottom pan of lightly salted water to a boil. Add the pasta, return to a boil, and cook for 8–10 minutes, or until tender but still firm to the bite.

Meanwhile, transfer the roasted vegetables to a large heavy-bottom pan and add the strained tomatoes and olives. Heat through gently, stirring occasionally. Drain the pasta and transfer to a warmed serving dish. Add the roasted vegetable sauce and toss well. Garnish with the fresh basil and parsley and serve immediately.

VARIATION
Other vegetables would work well in this dish, such as bite-size pieces of butternut squash, and cherry tomato halves.

serves 4 | prep 10 mins | cook 12 mins

bavettine with smoked salmon & arugula

Do not overcook the salmon or arugula; they should just be warmed through and the arugula lightly wilted. If arugula is unavailable, substitute it with baby spinach leaves.

INGREDIENTS
12 oz/350 g dried bavettine
2 tbsp olive oil
1 garlic clove, chopped finely
4 oz/115 g smoked salmon, cut into thin strips
2 oz/55 g arugula
salt and pepper
½ lemon, to garnish

Bring a large, heavy-bottom pan of lightly salted water to a boil. Add the pasta, return to a boil, and cook for 8–10 minutes, or until tender but still firm to the bite.

Just before the end of the cooking time, heat the olive oil in a heavy-bottom skillet. Add the garlic and cook over low heat, stirring constantly, for 1 minute. Do not allow the garlic to brown or it will taste bitter. Add the salmon and arugula. Season to taste with salt and pepper and cook, stirring constantly, for 1 minute. Remove the skillet from the heat.

Drain the pasta and transfer to a warmed serving dish. Add the smoked salmon and arugula mixture, toss lightly, and serve, garnished with a lemon half.

serves 4 | prep 15 mins | cook 1hr 15 mins

lasagna al forno

Layers of pasta, meat sauce, and lasagna, all covered with a rich cheese sauce, makes a tasty and substantial family supper.

INGREDIENTS
2 tbsp olive oil
2 oz/55 g pancetta or rindless
  lean bacon, chopped
1 onion, chopped
1 garlic clove, chopped finely
1 cup fresh ground beef
2 celery stalks, chopped
2 carrots, chopped
salt and pepper
pinch of sugar
½ tsp dried oregano
14 oz/400 g canned chopped tomatoes
8 oz/225 g dried no-precook lasagna
1 cup freshly grated Parmesan cheese,
  plus extra for sprinkling

cheese sauce
2 tsp Dijon mustard
2½ oz/70 g Cheddar cheese, grated
2½ oz/70 g Swiss cheese, grated
1¼ cups hot Béchamel Sauce
  (see page 27)

VARIATION
Substitute the Swiss cheese with another good melting cheese, such as Emmental, if you prefer.

Preheat the oven to 375°F/190°C. Heat the olive oil in a large, heavy-bottom pan. Add the pancetta and cook over medium heat, stirring occasionally, for 3 minutes, or until the fat starts to run. Add the onion and garlic and cook, stirring occasionally, for 5 minutes, or until softened.

Add the beef and cook, breaking it up with a wooden spoon, until browned all over. Stir in the celery and carrot and cook for 5 minutes. Season to taste with salt and pepper. Add the sugar, oregano, and tomatoes and their can juices. Bring to a boil, reduce the heat, and let simmer for 30 minutes.

Meanwhile, to make the cheese sauce, stir the mustard and both cheeses into the hot Béchamel Sauce.

In a large, rectangular heatproof dish, make alternate layers of meat sauce, lasagna, and Parmesan cheese. Pour the cheese sauce over the layers, covering them completely, and sprinkle with Parmesan cheese. Bake in the preheated oven for 30 minutes, or until golden brown and bubbling. Serve immediately.

serves 4 | prep 15 mins | cook 1 hr 25 mins

pork & pasta bake

When cooking with olive oil, there is no need to use extra virgin olive oil as the flavor will be lost during cooking. Olive oil is best stored in a cool place, out of direct sunlight. Do not store in the refrigerator.

INGREDIENTS
2 tbsp olive oil
1 onion, chopped
1 garlic clove,
  chopped finely
2 carrots, diced
2 oz/55 g pancetta
  or rindless lean bacon, chopped
4 oz/115 g mushrooms, chopped
1 lb/450 g ground pork
½ cup dry white wine
4 tbsp strained tomatoes
7 oz/200 g canned chopped tomatoes
2 tsp chopped fresh
  sage or ½ tsp dried sage
8 oz/225 g dried elicoidali
5 oz/140 g mozzarella cheese, diced
4 tbsp freshly grated Parmesan cheese
1¼ cups hot Béchamel Sauce (see page 27)
salt and pepper

Preheat the oven to 400°F/200°C. Heat the olive oil in a large, heavy-bottom skillet. Add the onion, garlic, and carrots and cook over low heat, stirring occasionally, for 5 minutes, or until the onion has softened. Add the pancetta and cook for 5 minutes. Add the chopped mushrooms and cook, stirring occasionally, for an additional 2 minutes. Add the pork and cook, breaking it up with a wooden spoon, until the meat is browned all over. Stir in the wine, strained tomatoes, chopped tomatoes and their can juices, and sage. Season to taste with salt and pepper and bring to a boil, then cover and simmer over low heat for 25–30 minutes.

Meanwhile, bring a large, heavy-bottom pan of lightly salted water to a boil. Add the pasta, return to a boil, and cook for 8–10 minutes, or until tender but still firm to the bite.

Spoon the pork mixture into a large heatproof dish. Stir the mozzarella and half the Parmesan cheese into the Béchamel Sauce. Drain the pasta and stir the sauce into it, then spoon it over the pork mixture. Sprinkle with the remaining Parmesan cheese and bake in the oven for 25–30 minutes, or until golden brown. Serve the bake immediately.

serves 4 | prep 15 mins | cook 1hr 40 mins

pasticcio

This recipe shares its origins with a traditional Greek bake made with lamb. It is delicious served hot or cold.

INGREDIENTS
1 tbsp olive oil
1 onion, chopped
2 garlic cloves, chopped finely
2 cups fresh ground lamb
2 tbsp tomato paste
2 tbsp all-purpose flour
1¼ cups Chicken Stock
  (see page 29)
salt and pepper
1 tsp ground cinnamon
4 oz/115 g dried short-cut macaroni
2 beefsteak tomatoes, sliced
1¼ cups strained plain yogurt
2 eggs, beaten lightly

Preheat the oven to 375°F/190°C. Heat the olive oil in a large heavy-bottom skillet. Add the onion and garlic and cook over low heat, stirring occasionally, for 5 minutes, or until softened. Add the lamb and cook, breaking it up with a wooden spoon, until browned all over. Add the tomato paste and sprinkle in the flour. Cook, stirring, for 1 minute, then stir in the Chicken Stock. Season to taste with salt and pepper and stir in the cinnamon. Bring to a boil, reduce the heat, cover, and cook for 25 minutes.

Meanwhile, bring a large heavy-bottom pan of lightly salted water to a boil. Add the pasta, return to a boil, and cook for 8–10 minutes, or until tender but still firm to the bite.

Spoon the lamb mixture into a large heat-proof dish and arrange the tomato slices on top. Drain the pasta and transfer to a bowl. Add the yogurt and eggs and mix well. Spoon the pasta mixture on top of the lamb and bake in the preheated oven for 1 hour. Serve immediately.

VARIATION
Pasticcio is also delicious made with fresh ground turkey or chicken. Replace the strained plain yogurt with plain yogurt, if you like.

serves 4 | prep 15 mins | cook 1hr 45 mins

chicken & wild mushroom cannelloni

Cannelloni tubes filled with a delicious mix of exotic mushrooms, chicken, and prosciutto make a wonderful dinner party main course. Serve with a crisp green salad, if you like.

INGREDIENTS
butter, for greasing
2 tbsp olive oil
2 garlic cloves, crushed
1 large onion, chopped finely
8 oz/225 g exotic mushrooms, sliced
1½ cups fresh ground chicken
4 oz/115 g prosciutto, diced
⅔ cup Marsala
7 oz/200 g canned chopped tomatoes
1 tbsp shredded fresh basil leaves
2 tbsp tomato paste
salt and pepper
10–12 cannelloni tubes
2½ cups Béchamel Sauce
   (see page 27)
¾ cup freshly grated
   Parmesan cheese

Preheat the oven to 375°F/190°C. Lightly grease a large heatproof dish. Heat the olive oil in a heavy-bottom skillet. Add the garlic, onion, and mushrooms, and cook over low heat, stirring frequently, for 8–10 minutes. Add the ground chicken and prosciutto and cook, stirring frequently, for 12 minutes, or until browned all over. Stir in the Marsala, tomatoes and their can juices, basil, and tomato paste, and cook for 4 minutes. Season to taste with salt and pepper, then cover and let simmer for 30 minutes. Uncover, stir, and let simmer for 15 minutes.

Meanwhile, bring a large heavy-bottom pan of lightly salted water to a boil. Add the pasta, return to a boil, and cook for 8–10 minutes, or until tender but still firm to the bite. Using a slotted spoon, transfer the cannelloni tubes to a plate and pat dry with paper towels.

Using a teaspoon, fill the cannelloni tubes with the chicken and mushroom mixture. Transfer them to the dish. Pour the Béchamel Sauce over them to cover completely and sprinkle with the grated Parmesan cheese.

Bake in the preheated oven for 30 minutes, or until golden brown and bubbling. Serve immediately.

VARIATION
If you like, replace the Marsala with the same quantity of brandy and substitute the canned tomatoes with the same amount of fresh tomatoes.

serves 4 | prep 20 mins | cook 1hr 5 mins

vegetarian lasagna

This variation on the traditional meat-filled lasagna will appeal to vegetarians and meat-eaters alike.

INGREDIENTS
olive oil, for brushing
2 eggplants, sliced
2 tbsp butter
1 garlic clove, chopped finely
4 zucchinis, sliced
1 tbsp finely chopped fresh flat-leaf parsley
1 tbsp finely chopped fresh marjoram
8 oz/225 g mozzarella cheese, grated
2½ cups strained tomatoes
175 g/6 oz dried no-precook lasagna
salt and pepper
2½ cups Béchamel Sauce
  (see page 27)
½ cup freshly grated
  Parmesan cheese

Preheat the oven to 400°F/200°C. Brush a large heatproof dish with olive oil. Brush a large grill pan with olive oil and heat until smoking. Add half the eggplant slices and cook over medium heat for 8 minutes, or until golden brown all over. Remove the eggplant from the grill pan and drain on paper towels. Add the remaining eggplant slices and extra oil, if necessary, and cook for 8 minutes, or until golden brown all over.

Melt the butter in a skillet and add the garlic, zucchinis, parsley, and marjoram. Cook over medium heat, stirring frequently, for 5 minutes, or until the zucchinis are golden brown all over. Remove from the skillet and let drain on paper towels.

Layer the eggplant, zucchinis, mozzarella, strained tomatoes, and lasagna in the dish, seasoning with salt and pepper as you go and finishing with a layer of lasagna. Pour over the Béchamel Sauce, making sure that all the pasta is covered. Sprinkle with the grated Parmesan cheese and bake in the preheated oven for 30–40 minutes, or until golden brown. Serve the lasagna immediately.

COOK'S TIP
Make sure that the oiled grill pan is very hot before adding the eggplant slices. Add extra oil if the eggplant is sticking to the pan.

serves 4 | prep 15 mins | cook 40 mins

baked pasta with mushrooms

A bake of pasta, béchamel sauce, and a tasty filling is sometimes called a crostata.

INGREDIENTS
5 oz/140 g fontina cheese, sliced thinly
1¼ cups hot Béchamel Sauce (see page 27)
6 tbsp butter, plus extra for greasing
12 oz/350 g mixed wild mushrooms, sliced
12 oz/350 g dried tagliatelle
2 egg yolks
4 tbsp freshly grated romano cheese
salt and pepper
mixed salad greens,
**   to serve**

Preheat the oven to 400°F/200°C. Stir the fontina cheese into the Béchamel Sauce and reserve.

Melt 2 tablespoons of the butter in a large pan. Add the mushrooms and cook over low heat, stirring occasionally, for 10 minutes.

Meanwhile, bring a large pan of lightly salted water to a boil. Add the pasta, return to a boil, and cook for 8–10 minutes, or until tender but still firm to the bite. Drain, return to the pan, and add the remaining butter, the egg yolks, and about one-third of the sauce, then season to taste with salt and pepper. Toss well to mix, then gently stir in the mushrooms.

Lightly grease a large, heatproof dish with butter and spoon in the pasta mixture. Pour over the remaining sauce evenly and sprinkle with the grated romano cheese. Bake in the preheated oven for 15–20 minutes, or until golden brown. Serve immediately with mixed salad greens.

serves 4 | prep 15 mins | cook 1hr 15 mins

sicilian spaghetti cake

This delicious classic dish of eggplants, tomatoes, meat, and olives is perfect for both a family midweek supper or a special occasion main course. Serve with a fresh green salad.

INGREDIENTS
½ cup olive oil
2 eggplants, sliced
1½ cups fresh ground beef
1 onion, chopped
2 garlic cloves, chopped finely
2 tbsp tomato paste
14 oz/400 g canned chopped tomatoes
1 tsp Worcestershire sauce
1 tbsp chopped fresh
　flat-leaf parsley
salt and pepper
⅓ cup pitted black olives, sliced
1 red bell pepper, seeded and chopped
6 oz/175 g dried spaghetti
1 cup freshly grated
　Parmesan cheese

Preheat the oven to 400°F/200°C. Brush an 8-inch/20-cm loose-bottom round cake pan with oil and line the bottom with parchment paper. Heat half the oil in a skillet. Add the eggplants in batches, and cook until lightly browned on both sides. Add more oil, as required. Drain the eggplants on paper towels, then arrange in overlapping slices to cover the bottom and sides of the cake pan, reserving a few slices.

Heat the remaining olive oil in a large pan and add the beef, onion, and garlic. Cook over medium heat, breaking up the meat with a wooden spoon, until browned all over. Add the tomato paste, tomatoes and their can juices, Worcestershire sauce, and parsley. Season to taste with salt and pepper and let simmer for 10 minutes. Add the olives and bell pepper and cook for 10 minutes.

Meanwhile, bring a pan of lightly salted water to a boil. Add the pasta, return to a boil, and cook for 8–10 minutes, or until tender but still firm to the bite. Drain and transfer to a bowl. Add the meat sauce and cheese and toss, then spoon into the cake pan, press down and cover with the remaining eggplant slices. Bake for 40 minutes. Let stand for 5 minutes, then loosen round the edges and invert onto a plate. Remove and discard the parchment paper and serve.

VARIATION
Other types of long pasta, such as linguine, also work well in this dish. Replace the red bell pepper with a yellow bell pepper, if you like.

serves 4 | prep 30 mins | cook 45 mins

seafood lasagna

You can use any type of white fish and any sauce you like in this recipe: try angler fish with whisky sauce or halibut with a cheese and parsley sauce.

INGREDIENTS
1 lb/450 g cod, filleted, skin
 removed and flesh flaked
4 oz/115 g shrimp
4 oz/115 g sole fillet, skin removed and
 flesh sliced
juice of 1 lemon
4 tbsp butter
3 leeks, sliced very thinly
scant ½ cup all-purpose flour
2⅓ cups milk
2 tbsp clear honey
2 cups grated mozzarella cheese
1 lb/450 g pre-cooked lasagna
⅔ cup freshly grated Parmesan cheese
pepper

VARIATION
For a hard cider sauce, substitute 1 finely chopped shallot for the leeks, 1½ cups cider and 1½ cups heavy cream for the milk, and 1 teaspoon of mustard for the honey. For a Tuscan sauce, substitute 1 chopped fennel bulb for the leeks and omit the honey.

Put the cod fillet, shrimp, and sole fillet into a large bowl and season with pepper and lemon juice according to taste. Set aside while you make the sauce.

Melt the butter in a large pan. Add the leeks and cook over low heat, stirring occasionally, for about 8 minutes until softened. Add the flour and cook, stirring constantly, for 1 minute. Gradually stir in enough milk to make a thick, creamy sauce.

Blend in the honey and mozzarella and cook for a further 3 minutes. Remove the pan from the heat and mix in the fish and shrimp.

Make alternate layers of fish sauce and lasagna in a heatproof dish, finishing with a layer of fish sauce on top. Generously sprinkle over the grated Parmesan cheese and bake in a preheated oven, 350°F/180°C, for 30 minutes. Serve immediately.

serves 4 | prep 10 mins | cook 1hr 5 mins

traditional cannelloni

More delicately flavored than the usual beef-filled cannelloni, this is still a substantial dish for a family supper.

INGREDIENTS
2 tbsp olive oil
2 onions, chopped
2 garlic cloves, chopped finely
1 tbsp shredded fresh basil
1 lb 12 oz/800 g canned
  chopped tomatoes
1 tbsp tomato paste
salt and pepper
12 oz/350 g dried cannelloni tubes
butter, for greasing
generous 1 cup ricotta cheese
4 oz/115 g cooked ham, diced
1 egg
½ cup freshly grated
  romano cheese

Preheat the oven to 350°F/180°C. Heat the olive oil in a large heavy-bottom skillet. Add the onions and garlic and cook over low heat, stirring occasionally, for 5 minutes, or until the onion is softened. Add the basil, chopped tomatoes and their can juices, and tomato paste, and season to taste with salt and pepper. Reduce the heat and let simmer for 30 minutes, or until thickened.

Meanwhile, bring a large heavy-bottom pan of lightly salted water to a boil. Add the cannelloni tubes, return to a boil, and cook for 8–10 minutes, or until tender but still firm to the bite. Using a slotted spoon, transfer the cannelloni tubes to a large plate and pat dry with paper towels.

Grease a large, shallow heatproof dish with butter. Mix the ricotta, ham, and egg together in a bowl and season to taste with salt and pepper. Using a teaspoon, fill the cannelloni tubes with the ricotta mixture and place in a single layer in the dish. Pour the tomato sauce over the cannelloni and sprinkle with the grated romano cheese. Bake in the preheated oven for 30 minutes, or until golden brown. Serve immediately.

VARIATION
Substitute the romano cheese with the same amount of freshly grated Parmesan cheese, if you prefer.

serves 4 | prep 1hr 15 mins | cook 25 mins

tortelloni

These tasty little squares of pasta stuffed with mushrooms and cheese are surprisingly filling. This recipe makes 36 tortelloni.

INGREDIENTS
about 10½ oz/300 g Basic Pasta Dough
  (see page 25), rolled out to thin sheets
5 tbsp butter
1¾ oz/50 g shallots, chopped finely
3 garlic cloves, crushed
1¾ oz/50 g mushrooms, wiped and
  chopped finely
½ stick celery, chopped finely
1 oz/25 g pecorino cheese, grated finely,
  plus extra to garnish
1 tbsp oil
salt and pepper

Using a serrated pasta cutter, cut 2-inch/5-cm squares from the sheets of fresh pasta. To make 36 tortelloni you will need 72 squares. Once the pasta is cut, cover the squares with plastic wrap to stop them drying out.

Heat 3 tablespoons of the butter in a skillet. Add the shallots, 1 crushed garlic clove, the mushrooms, and the celery and cook for 4–5 minutes.

Remove the skillet from the heat, stir in the cheese and season with salt and pepper to taste.

Spoon ½ teaspoon of the mixture onto the middle of 36 pasta squares. Brush the edges of the squares with water and top with the remaining 36 squares. Press the edges together to seal. Let rest for at least 5 minutes.

Bring a large pan of water to a boil, add the oil, and cook the tortelloni, in batches, for 2–3 minutes. The tortelloni will rise to the surface when cooked and the pasta should be tender with a slight «bite.» Remove from the pan with a slotted spoon and drain thoroughly.

Meanwhile, melt the remaining butter in a pan. Add the remaining garlic and plenty of pepper and cook for 1–2 minutes. Transfer the tortelloni to serving plates and pour over the garlic butter. Garnish with grated pecorino cheese and serve immediately.

serves 4 | prep 25 mins | cook 50 mins

green easter pie

*This traditional Easter risotto pie is from
Piedmont in northern Italy.
Serve it warm or chilled in slices.*

INGREDIENTS
3 oz/80 g arugula
2 tbsp olive oil
1 onion, chopped
2 garlic cloves, chopped
7 oz/200 g risotto rice
scant 3 cups hot Chicken or Vegetable Stock
   (see page 29)
scant ½ cup white wine
1¾ oz/50 g Parmesan cheese, grated
3½ oz/100 g frozen peas, defrosted
2 tomatoes, diced
4 eggs, beaten
3 tbsp fresh marjoram, chopped
1¾ oz/50 g bread crumbs
salt and pepper

Lightly grease and then line the base of
a 9-inch/23-cm deep cake pan.

Using a sharp knife, roughly chop the
arugula and set aside.

Heat the oil in a large skillet. Add the onion
and garlic and cook for 4–5 minutes or until
softened.

Add the rice to the mixture in the skillet,
mix well to combine, then begin adding the
stock a ladleful at a time. Wait until all of
the stock has been absorbed before adding
another ladleful of liquid.

Continue to cook the mixture, adding the
wine, until the rice is tender. This will take
at least 15 minutes.

Stir in the Parmesan cheese, peas, arugula,
tomatoes, eggs, and 2 tablespoons of
the marjoram. Season to taste with salt and
pepper.

Spoon the risotto into the pan and level the
surface by pressing down with the back of
a wooden spoon.

Top with the bread crumbs and the
remaining marjoram.

Bake in a preheated oven, at 350°F/180°C,
for 30 minutes or until set. Cut the pie into
slices and serve immediately.

serves 6 | prep 10 mins + 30 mins soaking | cook 40 mins

sunshine risotto

Romano is an Italian cheese made from sheep milk. Although it is made all over Italy, the aged romano from Sardinia is particularly fine.

INGREDIENTS
about 12 sun-dried tomatoes
generous 6⅓ cups Chicken or Vegetable Stock
   (see page 29)
2 tbsp olive oil
1 large onion,
   chopped finely
4–6 garlic cloves,
   chopped finely
generous 1¾ cups
   risotto rice
2 tbsp chopped fresh
   flat-leaf parsley
1 cup freshly grated aged romano cheese
extra virgin olive oil,
   for drizzling

Place the sun-dried tomatoes in a heatproof bowl and pour over enough boiling water to cover. Set aside to soak for 30 minutes, or until soft and supple. Drain and pat dry with paper towels, then shred thinly and set aside.

Bring the stock to a boil in a pan, then reduce the heat and keep simmering gently over low heat until you are ready to add it to the risotto.

Heat the olive oil in a deep pan over medium heat. Add the onion and cook, stirring occasionally, for 2 minutes, or until starting to soften. Add the garlic and cook for an additional 15 seconds.

Reduce the heat, add the rice, and mix to coat in oil. Cook, stirring constantly, for 2–3 minutes, or until the grains are translucent.

Gradually add the hot stock, a ladleful at a time. Stir constantly, adding more liquid as the rice absorbs each addition. Increase the heat to medium so that the liquid bubbles. After approximately 15 minutes, stir in the sun-dried tomatoes.

Continue adding the stock, stirring constantly, until the risotto has been cooking for 20 minutes, or until all the liquid is absorbed and the rice is creamy.

Remove the pan from the heat and stir in the chopped parsley and half the romano cheese. Spoon the risotto onto 6 warmed plates. Drizzle with extra virgin olive oil and sprinkle the remaining romano cheese on top. Serve at once.

serves 6 | prep 15 mins | cook 35 mins

minted green risotto

This tasty risotto gets its vibrant green color from the spinach and mint. Serve with Italian-style rustic bread and salad for an informal supper.

INGREDIENTS
4 cups Chicken or Vegetable Stock
   (see page 29)
2 tbsp butter
generous 1½ cups shelled fresh peas or
   thawed frozen peas
5⅝ cups fresh young spinach leaves, washed
   and drained
1 bunch of fresh mint, leaves stripped from
   stalks
2 tbsp chopped fresh basil
2 tbsp chopped fresh oregano
pinch of freshly grated nutmeg
4 tbsp mascarpone cheese or heavy cream
2 tbsp vegetable oil
1 onion, chopped finely
2 celery stalks, including leaves,
   chopped finely
2 garlic cloves, chopped finely
½ tsp dried thyme
scant 1½ cups risotto rice
¼ cup dry white vermouth
¾ cup freshly grated Parmesan cheese

Bring the stock to a boil in a pan, then reduce the heat and keep simmering gently over low heat while you are cooking the risotto.

Heat half the butter in a deep skillet over medium-high heat until sizzling. Add the peas, spinach, mint leaves, basil, and oregano and season with the nutmeg. Cook, stirring frequently, for 3 minutes, or until the spinach and mint leaves are wilted. Let cool slightly.

Pour the spinach mixture into a food processor and process for 15 seconds. Add the mascarpone and process again for 1 minute. Transfer to a bowl and set aside.

Heat the oil and remaining butter in a large, heavy-bottom pan over medium heat. Add the onion, celery, garlic, and thyme and cook, stirring occasionally, for 2 minutes, or until the vegetables are softened.

Reduce the heat, add the rice, and mix to coat in oil and butter. Cook, stirring constantly, for 2–3 minutes, or until the grains are translucent. Add the vermouth and cook, stirring constantly, until it has reduced.

Gradually add the hot stock, a ladleful at a time. Stir constantly and add more liquid as the rice absorbs each addition. Increase the heat to medium so that the liquid bubbles. Cook for 20 minutes, or until the liquid is absorbed and the rice is creamy.

Stir in the spinach-mascarpone mixture and the Parmesan. Transfer to warmed plates and serve at once.

VARIATION
If you don't have any vermouth, you can substitute the same quantity of dry white wine.

serves 4 | prep 15 mins | cook 35 mins

rice & peas

This famous and rather pretty dish is one of many risotti from the Veneto.

INGREDIENTS
4 cups Vegetable Stock (see page 29)
3 oz/85 g butter
3 shallots, chopped finely
4 oz/115 g pancetta or rindless
    lean bacon, diced
scant 1¼ cups rice
⅔ cup dry white wine
1½ cups petits pois, thawed if using frozen
salt and pepper
Parmesan cheese shavings, to garnish

Pour the stock into a large pan and bring to a boil. Reduce the heat and let simmer gently while you are cooking the risotto.

Melt 2 oz/55 g of the butter in another large, heavy-bottom pan. Add the shallots and pancetta and cook over low heat, stirring occasionally, for 5 minutes, until the shallots are softened. Add the rice and cook, stirring constantly, for 2–3 minutes, until all the grains are thoroughly coated and glistening.

Pour in the wine and cook, stirring constantly, until it has almost completely evaporated. Add a ladleful of hot stock and cook, stirring constantly, until all the stock has been absorbed. Continue cooking and adding the stock, a ladleful at a time, for about 10 minutes.

Add the peas, then continue adding the stock, a ladleful at a time, for an additional 10 minutes, or until the rice is tender and the liquid has been absorbed.

Stir in the remaining butter and season to taste with salt and pepper. Transfer to a warmed serving dish, garnish with Parmesan shavings, and serve immediately.

VARIATION
You can substitute diced cooked ham for the pancetta or bacon and add it toward the end of the cooking time so that it heats through.

serves 2 | prep 20 mins | cook 1 hr

rice-filled eggplants

An eggplant is halved and filled with a risotto mixture, topped with cheese, and then baked to make a snack or quick meal for two.

INGREDIENTS
¼ cup mixed long-grain and
  wild rice
1 eggplant, about 12 oz/350 g
1 tbsp olive oil
1 small onion, chopped finely
1 garlic clove, crushed
½ small red bell pepper, cored, seeded,
  and chopped
2 tbsp water
3 tbsp raisins
¼ cup cashew nuts,
  chopped roughly
½ tsp dried oregano
⅓ cup sharp Cheddar or Parmesan cheese,
  grated
salt and pepper
fresh oregano or parsley, to garnish

Cook the rice in a pan of boiling salted water for 15 minutes or until tender. Drain, rinse, and drain again.

Bring a large pan of water to a boil. Cut the stem off the eggplant and then cut in half lengthwise. Cut out the flesh from the center, leaving a ½-inch/1.5-cm shell. Blanch the shells in the boiling water for 3–4 minutes. Drain, then chop the eggplant flesh finely.

Heat the oil in a pan and fry the onion and garlic gently until just beginning to soften.

Add the bell pepper and eggplant flesh and continue cooking for 2 minutes. Add the water and cook for 2–3 minutes.

Stir the raisins, cashew nuts, oregano, and rice into the eggplant mixture and season with salt and pepper to taste.

Lay the eggplant shells in a heatproof dish and spoon in the rice mixture, piling it up well. Cover and place in a preheated oven, at 375°F/190°C, for 20 minutes.

Remove the dish from the oven, take off the lid, and sprinkle the cheese over the rice. Place under a preheated moderate broiler for 3–4 minutes or until golden brown. Serve the filled eggplants hot, garnished with oregano or parsley.

serves 4 | prep 15 mins | cook 35 mins

chicken risotto with saffron

The possibilities for this risotto are endless—try adding the following just at the end of cooking time: cashews and corn, lightly sautéed zucchinis and basil, or artichokes and oyster mushrooms.

INGREDIENTS
generous 5½ cups Chicken Stock
  (see page 29)
4½ oz/125 g butter
2 lb/900 g skinless, boneless chicken breasts,
  sliced thinly
1 large onion, chopped
1 lb 2 oz/500 g risotto rice
⅔ cup white wine
1 tsp crumbled saffron threads
½ cup freshly grated Parmesan cheese
salt and pepper

Bring the stock to a boil in a pan, then reduce the heat and simmer gently over low heat while you are cooking the risotto.

Meanwhile, heat 2 oz/55 g of the butter in a deep pan, add the chicken and onion, and cook, stirring frequently, for 8 minutes, or until golden brown.

Add the rice and mix to coat in the butter. Cook, stirring constantly for 2–3 minutes, or until the grains are translucent. Add the wine and cook, stirring constantly, for 1 minute until reduced.

Mix the saffron with 4 tablespoons of the hot stock. Add the liquid to the rice and cook, stirring constantly, until it is absorbed.

Gradually add the remaining hot stock, a ladleful at a time. Stir constantly and add more liquid as the rice absorbs each addition. Cook for 20 minutes, or until all the liquid is absorbed and the rice is creamy. Season to taste.

Remove the risotto from the heat and add the remaining butter. Mix well, then stir in the Parmesan until it melts. Spoon the risotto onto warmed plates and serve at once.

serves 4 | prep 15 mins | cook 35 mins

shredded spinach & ham risotto

For a spicier flavor, you could substitute salami for the ham. Make sure that you peel off any rind before cutting the slices into strips.

INGREDIENTS
5 cups fresh young spinach leaves
4 oz/115 g cooked ham
4 cups Chicken Stock
  (see page 29)
1 tbsp olive oil
3 tbsp butter
1 small onion, finely chopped
generous 1⅜ cups risotto rice
⅔ cup dry white wine
¼ cup light cream
¼ cup freshly grated Parmesan or Grana
  Padano cheese
salt and pepper

Wash the spinach well and slice into thin shreds. Cut the ham into thin strips.

Bring the stock to a boil in a pan, then reduce the heat and keep simmering gently over low heat while you are cooking the risotto.

Heat the oil with 2 tablespoons of the butter in a deep pan over medium heat until the butter has melted. Add the onion and cook, stirring occasionally, for 5 minutes, or until soft and starting to turn golden. Do not brown.

Reduce the heat, add the rice, and mix to coat in oil and butter. Cook, stirring constantly, for 2–3 minutes, or until the grains are translucent.

Add the wine and cook, stirring constantly, for 1 minute until reduced.

Gradually add the hot stock, a ladleful at a time. Stir constantly and add more liquid as the rice absorbs each addition. Increase the heat to medium so that the liquid bubbles. Cook for 20 minutes, or until all the liquid is absorbed and the rice is creamy. Add the spinach and ham with the last ladleful of stock.

Remove the risotto from the heat and add the remaining butter and the cream. Mix well, then stir in the Parmesan until it melts. Season to taste and serve at once.

serves 4 | prep 1hr 15 mins + 1 hr chilling | cook 45 mins

gnocchi romana

This is a traditional Italian recipe but, for a less rich version, simply omit the eggs.

INGREDIENTS
3⅛ cups milk
pinch of freshly grated nutmeg
6 tbsp butter, plus extra
 for greasing
1¼ cups semolina
1½ cups grated
 Parmesan cheese
2 eggs, beaten
½ cup grated Swiss cheese
salt and pepper
fresh basil sprigs, to garnish

Pour the milk into a pan and bring to a boil. Remove the pan from the heat and stir in the nutmeg, 2 tablespoons of butter, and salt and pepper.

Gradually stir the semolina into the milk, whisking to prevent lumps forming, and return the pan to a low heat. Simmer, stirring constantly, for about 10 minutes, or until very thick.

Beat ⅔ cup of Parmesan cheese into the semolina mixture, then beat in the eggs. Continue beating the mixture until smooth. Set the mixture aside for a few minutes to cool slightly.

Spread out the cooled semolina mixture in an even layer on a sheet of baking parchment or in a large, oiled baking pan, smoothing the surface with a damp spatula—it should be ½ inch/1 cm thick. Set aside to cool completely, then chill in the refrigerator for 1 hour.

Once chilled, cut out rounds of gnocchi, measuring about 1½ inches/4 cm in diameter, using a plain, greased pastry cutter.

Grease a shallow heatproof dish or 4 individual dishes. Lay the gnocchi trimmings in the base of the dish or dishes and cover with overlapping rounds of gnocchi.

Melt the remaining butter and drizzle over the gnocchi. Sprinkle over the remaining Parmesan, then sprinkle over the Swiss cheese.

Bake in a preheated oven, at 400°F/200°C, for 25–30 minutes, until the top is crisp and golden brown. Serve hot, garnished with the basil sprigs.

serves 4 | prep 30 mins + 1 hr chilling | cook 15 mins

spinach & ricotta gnocchi

These mouthwatering dumplings, made with spinach and ricotta cheese are best served simply, coated in a herb butter and sprinkled with Parmesan cheese.

INGREDIENTS
2 lb 4 oz/1 kg fresh spinach, coarse stalks
  removed
1½ cups ricotta cheese
1 cup freshly grated Parmesan cheese
3 eggs, beaten lightly
pinch of freshly grated nutmeg
salt and pepper
generous ¾ cup all-purpose flour, plus extra
  for dusting

for the herb butter
4 oz/115 g unsalted butter
2 tbsp chopped fresh oregano
2 tbsp chopped fresh sage

Wash the spinach, and place it in a pan. Cover and cook over low heat for 6–8 minutes, until just wilted. Drain well and set aside to cool.

Squeeze or press out as much liquid as possible from the spinach, then chop finely or process in a food processor or blender. Place the spinach in a bowl and add the ricotta, half the Parmesan, the eggs, and nutmeg, and season to taste with salt and pepper. Beat until thoroughly combined. Start by sifting in ¾ cup of the flour and lightly work it into the mixture, adding more, if necessary, to make a workable mixture. Cover with plastic wrap and let chill for 1 hour.

With floured hands, break off small pieces of the mixture and roll them into walnut-size balls. Handle them as little as possible, as they are quite delicate. Lightly dust the dumplings with flour.

Bring a large pan of lightly salted water to a boil. Add the dumplings and cook for 2–3 minutes, until they rise to the surface. Remove them from the pan with a slotted spoon, drain well, and set aside.

Meanwhile, make the herb butter. Melt the butter in a heavy-bottom skillet. Add the oregano and sage and cook over low heat, stirring frequently, for 1 minute. Add the dumplings, toss for 1 minute to coat, and transfer to a warm serving dish. Sprinkle with the remaining Parmesan, and serve.

serves 4 | prep 30 mins + 1 hr chilling | cook 40 mins

basil dumplings

While gnocchi are traditionally served in Italy as a primo or first course, they can also make an unusual and delicious accompaniment to meat or fish.

INGREDIENTS
3 cups milk
1¾ cups semolina
1 tbsp finely chopped fresh basil leaves
4 sun-dried tomatoes in oil, drained and chopped finely
2 eggs, beaten lightly
2 oz/55 g butter, plus extra for greasing
¾ cup freshly grated Parmesan cheese
salt and pepper
Basic Tomato Sauce (see page 26), to serve

Pour the milk into a large pan and bring to just below boiling point. Sprinkle in the semolina, stirring constantly. Reduce the heat and let simmer gently for about 2 minutes, until thick and smooth. Remove the pan from the heat.

Stir in the basil, sun-dried tomatoes, eggs, half the butter, and half the Parmesan, and season to taste with salt and pepper. Stir well until all the ingredients are thoroughly incorporated, then pour into a shallow dish or baking sheet and level the surface. Set aside to cool, then let chill for at least 1 hour, until set.

Lightly grease a heatproof dish with butter. Using a lightly floured, plain round cutter, stamp out circles of the set semolina mixture. Place the trimmings in the bottom of the dish and top with the circles.

Melt the remaining butter and brush it over the semolina circles, then sprinkle with the remaining Parmesan. Bake in a preheated oven, 375°F/190°C, for 30–35 minutes, until golden. Serve immediately with Basic Tomato Sauce.

part three

SECONDI PIATTI
meat, poultry, game, fish & seafood, vegetable main courses

The meat and poultry eaten in Italy is lean and

tender, the seafood is fresh, and so are the

vegetables. With all these ingredients, it is the

quality, not the quantity that is the key to the

main course in Italy, and the recipes in this chapter

represent the very best of Italy's main courses.

serves 4 | prep 15 mins | cook 3 hrs 30 mins

beef in red wine

Apart from producing what is arguably the best olive oil in the world, Tuscany is renowned for producing quite simple dishes in which the flavors are perfectly harmonized. This is one of them.

INGREDIENTS
2 lb 12 oz/1.25 kg topside of beef
salt and pepper
3 tbsp olive oil
1 red onion, chopped
1 garlic clove, chopped finely
2 carrots, sliced
2 celery stalks, sliced
1¼ cups Chianti
7 oz/200 g canned tomatoes, chopped
1 tbsp chopped fresh oregano
1 tbsp chopped fresh flat-leaf parsley
1 bay leaf

Season the beef all over with salt and pepper. Heat the olive oil in a large, flame-proof casserole. Add the beef and cook over medium heat, turning frequently, until browned on all sides. Use 2 large forks to remove the beef from the casserole.

Reduce the heat, add the onion, garlic, carrots, and celery, and cook, stirring occasionally, for 5 minutes, until softened. Pour in the wine and add the tomatoes, oregano, parsley, and bay leaf. Stir well to mix and bring to a boil.

Return the meat to the casserole and spoon the vegetable mixture over it. Cover and cook in a preheated oven, 350°F/180°C, spooning the vegetables over the meat occasionally, for 3–3¼ hours, until the beef is tender.

Transfer the beef to a carving board and cover with foil. Place the casserole on high heat and bring the juices to a boil. Continue to boil until reduced and thickened.

Carve the beef into slices and place on a warmed serving platter. Strain the thickened cooking juices over the beef and serve immediately.

serves 4 | prep 10 mins | cook 26 mins

pizzaiola steak

Originating in Naples, where it is difficult to find any dish that does not feature the brilliantly colored, rich-tasting tomatoes of the region, this way of serving steak is now popular throughout Italy—and beyond.

COOK'S TIP
*To peel tomatoes, place them in a heatproof bowl, pour boiling water over them, and soak for 3–4 minutes. When cool enough to handle make a cross in the base of each tomato with a sharp knife—the skins will peel away easily.

INGREDIENTS
3 tbsp olive oil, plus extra for brushing
1 lb 9 oz/700 g tomatoes, peeled* and
    chopped
1 red bell pepper, seeded and chopped
1 onion, chopped
2 garlic cloves, chopped finely
1 tbsp chopped fresh flat-leaf parsley
1 tsp dried oregano
1 tsp sugar
salt and pepper
4 x 6 oz/175 g entrecôte or rump steaks

Place the oil, tomatoes, red bell pepper, onion, garlic, parsley, oregano, and sugar in a heavy-bottom pan and season to taste with salt and pepper. Bring to a boil, reduce the heat and let simmer for 15 minutes.

Meanwhile, snip any fat round the outsides of the steaks. Season each generously with pepper (but no salt) and brush with olive oil. Cook on a very hot preheated grill pan for 1 minute on each side. Reduce the heat to medium and cook according to taste: 1½–2 minutes each side for rare; 2½–3 minutes each side for medium; 3–4 minutes on each side for well done.

Transfer the steaks to warmed individual plates and spoon the sauce over them. Serve immediately.

serves 6 | prep 35 mins | cook 1 hr 30 mins

layered meat loaf

The hidden pasta layer comes as a pleasant surprise inside this lightly spiced meat loaf.

INGREDIENTS
2 tbsp butter, plus extra
  for greasing
1 small onion, chopped finely
1 small red bell pepper, cored, seeded,
  and chopped
1 garlic clove, chopped
4 cups ground beef
½ cup white bread crumbs
½ tsp cayenne pepper
1 tbsp lemon juice
½ tsp grated lemon rind
2 tbsp chopped fresh parsley
¾ cup dried short pasta,
  such as fusilli
1 tbsp olive oil
1 cup Béchamel Sauce (see page 27)
4 bay leaves
6 oz/175 g fatty bacon, rinds removed
salt and pepper
salad greens, to serve

Melt the butter in a skillet over medium heat and fry the onion and bell pepper for about 3 minutes. Stir in the garlic and cook for 1 minute or until soft.

Put the meat into a bowl and mash with a wooden spoon until sticky. Add the onion mixture, bread crumbs, cayenne pepper, lemon juice, lemon rind, and parsley. Season and set aside.

Bring a pan of salted water to a boil. Add the pasta and oil and cook for 8–10 minutes, until almost tender. Drain and stir into the Béchamel Sauce.

Grease a 2 lb 4-oz/1-kg loaf pan and arrange the bay leaves in the base. Stretch the bacon slices with the back of a knife and line the base and sides of the pan with them. Spoon in half the meat mixture and smooth the surface. Cover with the pasta mixed with Béchamel Sauce, then spoon in the remaining meat mixture. Level the top and cover with foil.

Bake the meat loaf in a preheated oven, at 350°F/180°C, for 1 hour or until the juices run clear when a skewer is inserted into the center and the loaf has shrunk away from the sides. Pour off any fat and turn out the loaf onto a serving dish. Serve with salad greens.

VARIATION
Add 2 tablespoons of grated Parmesan cheese to the Béchamel Sauce before adding the pasta.

serves 4 | prep 45 mins | cook 1 hr 45 mins

rich beef stew

This slow-cooked beef stew is flavored with the flesh and rind of oranges, red wine, and porcini mushrooms.

INGREDIENTS
1 tbsp oil
1 tbsp butter
8 oz/225 g baby onions, peeled and halved
1 lb 5 oz/600 g stewing steak, diced into
   1½-inch/4-cm chunks
1¼ cups beef stock
⅔ cup red wine
4 tbsp chopped oregano
1 tbsp sugar
1 orange
1 oz/25 g porcini or other dried mushrooms
8 oz/225 g fresh plum tomatoes
cooked rice or potatoes, to serve

Heat the oil and butter in a large skillet. Add the onions and sauté for 5 minutes or until golden. Remove the onions with a slotted spoon, set aside, and keep warm.

Add the beef to the skillet and cook, stirring, for 5 minutes or until browned all over.

Return the onions to the skillet and add the stock, wine, oregano, and sugar, stirring to mix well. Transfer the mixture to a heatproof casserole dish.

Pare the rind from the orange and cut it into strips. Slice the orange flesh into rings. Add the orange rings and the rind to the casserole. Cook in a preheated oven, at 350°F/180°C, for 1¼ hours.

Soak the porcini mushrooms for 30 minutes in a small bowl containing 4 tablespoons of warm water.

Peel and halve the tomatoes. Add the tomatoes, porcini mushrooms, and their soaking liquid to the casserole. Cook for a further 20 minutes until the beef is tender and the juices thickened. Serve with cooked rice or potatoes.

COOK'S TIP
If fresh plum tomatoes are unavailable use the canned whole variety rather than another variety of fresh tomato.

serves 4 | prep 30 mins + 1 hr chilling | cook 6 mins

pan-fried pork with mozzarella

Although many cities are snapping at Rome's heels for the title of gastronomic capital of Italy, the Eternal City still wears the crown.

INGREDIENTS
1 lb/450 g loin of pork
2–3 garlic cloves, chopped finely
6 oz/175 g mozzarella cheese, drained
salt and pepper
12 slices prosciutto
12 fresh sage leaves
2 oz/55 g unsalted butter
mostarda di Verona,* to serve (optional)

to garnish
flat-leaf parsley sprigs
lemon slices

Trim any excess fat from the meat, then slice it crosswise into 12 pieces, each about 1 inch/2.5 cm thick. Stand each piece on end and beat with the flat end of a meat mallet or the side of a rolling pin until thoroughly flattened. Rub each piece all over with garlic, transfer to a plate, and cover with plastic wrap. Set aside in a cool place for 30 minutes to 1 hour.

Cut the mozzarella into 12 slices. Season the pork to taste with salt and pepper, then place a slice of cheese on top of each slice of meat. Top with a slice of prosciutto, letting it fall in folds. Place a sage leaf on each portion and secure with a toothpick.

Melt the butter in a large, heavy-bottom skillet. Add the pork, in batches if necessary, and cook for 2–3 minutes on each side, until the meat is tender and the cheese has melted. Remove with a slotted spoon and keep warm while you cook the remaining batch.

Remove and discard the toothpicks. Transfer the pork to 4 warmed individual plates, garnish with parsley and lemon slices, and serve immediately with mostarda di Verona.

COOK'S TIP
Mostarda di Verona is made with apple purée and is available from some good Italian delicatessens.

serves 4 | prep 20 mins | cook 12 mins

pork fillets with fennel

This is a very rich dish with a creamy Gorgonzola sauce that provides a perfect balance for the aniseed flavor of the fennel and the Italian liqueur, Sambuca.

INGREDIENTS
1 lb/450 g pork fillet
2–3 tbsp virgin olive oil
2 tbsp Sambuca liqueur
1 large fennel bulb, sliced, fronds reserved
3 oz/85 g Gorgonzola cheese, crumbled
2 tbsp light cream
1 tbsp chopped fresh sage
1 tbsp chopped fresh thyme
salt and pepper

Trim any fat from the pork and cut into ¼-inch/5-mm thick slices. Place the slices between 2 sheets of plastic wrap and beat with the flat end of a meat mallet or with a rolling pin to flatten slightly.

Heat 2 tablespoons of the oil in a heavy-bottom skillet and add the pork, in batches. Cook over medium heat for 2–3 minutes on each side, until tender. Remove from the skillet and keep warm. Cook the remaining batches, adding more oil if necessary.

Stir the Sambuca into the skillet, increase the heat, and cook, stirring constantly and scraping up the glazed bits from the bottom. Add the fennel and cook, stirring and turning frequently, for 3 minutes. Remove the fennel from the skillet and keep warm.

Reduce the heat, add the Gorgonzola and cream, and cook, stirring constantly, until smooth. Remove the skillet from the heat, stir in the sage and thyme, and season to taste with salt and pepper.

Divide the pork and fennel between 4 warmed individual serving plates and pour over the sauce. Garnish with the reserved fennel fronds and serve immediately.

serves 4 | prep 25 mins | cook 1 hr

pork with lemon & garlic

This is a simplified version of a traditional dish from the Marche region of Italy. Pork fillet pockets are stuffed with prosciutto and herbs.

INGREDIENTS
1 lb/450 g pork fillet
1¾ oz/50 g chopped almonds
2 tbsp olive oil
3½ oz/100 g raw prosciutto di Parma,
  chopped finely
2 garlic cloves, chopped
1 tbsp fresh oregano, chopped
finely grated rind of 2 lemons
4 shallots, chopped finely
¾ cup Chicken Stock (see page 29)
1 tsp sugar

Using a sharp knife, cut the pork fillet into 4 equal pieces. Place the pork between sheets of waxed paper and pound each piece with a meat mallet or the end of a rolling pin to flatten it.

Cut a horizontal slit in each piece of pork to make a pocket.

Place the almonds on a cookie sheet. Lightly toast the almonds under a medium-hot broiler for 2–3 minutes or until golden.

Mix the almonds with 1 tablespoon of oil, the prosciutto, garlic, oregano, and the finely grated rind of 1 lemon. Spoon the mixture into the pockets of the pork.

Heat the remaining oil in a large skillet. Add the shallots and cook for 2 minutes or until soft.

Add the pork to the skillet and cook for 2 minutes on each side or until the pork is browned all over.

Add the stock to the skillet, bring to a boil, cover, and let simmer for 45 minutes or until the pork is tender. Remove the meat from the skillet, set aside, and keep warm.

Add the lemon rind and sugar to the skillet, boil for 3–4 minutes or until reduced and syrupy. Pour the lemon sauce over the pork fillets and serve immediately.

serves 6 | prep 25 mins | cook 2 hrs 45 mins

slow-roasted pork

This wonderfully succulent roast from Perugia may be served hot with green beans or peperonata or cold with a crisp green salad.

COOK'S TIP
*Ready-prepared boned and rolled loin of pork is available from supermarkets and butchers, or you can ask your butcher to prepare one for you.

INGREDIENTS
3 lb 8 oz/1.6 kg loin of pork, boned and rolled*
4 garlic cloves, sliced thinly lengthwise
1½ tsp finely chopped fresh fennel fronds or ½ tsp dried fennel
4 cloves
salt and pepper
1¼ cups dry white wine
1¼ cups water

Use a small, sharp knife to make incisions all over the pork, opening them out slightly to make little pockets. Place the garlic slices in a small strainer and rinse under cold running water to moisten. Spread out the fennel on a saucer and roll the garlic slices in it to coat. Slide the garlic slices and the cloves into the pockets in the pork. Season the meat all over with salt and pepper.

Place the pork in a large heatproof dish or roasting pan. Pour in the wine and water. Cook in a preheated oven, 300°F/150°C, basting the meat occasionally, for 2½–2¾ hours, until the pork is tender but still quite moist.

If you are serving the pork hot, transfer it to a carving board and cut into slices. If you are serving it cold, let it cool completely in the cooking juices before removing and slicing.

serves 4 | prep 15 mins | cook 50 mins

roman pan-fried lamb

Chunks of tender lamb, pan-fried with garlic and stewed in red wine is a real Roman dish.

INGREDIENTS
1 tbsp oil
1 tbsp butter
1 lb 5 oz/600 g lamb (shoulder or leg),
    cut into 1-inch/2.5-cm chunks
4 garlic cloves, peeled
3 sprigs thyme, stalks removed
6 canned anchovy fillets
⅔ cup red wine
⅔ cup Vegetable Stock (see page 29)
1 tsp sugar
1¾ oz/50 g black olives, pitted and halved
2 tbsp chopped parsley, to garnish
creamed potato, to serve

Heat the oil and butter in a large skillet. Add the lamb and cook for 4–5 minutes, stirring, until the meat is browned all over.

Using a pestle and mortar, grind together the garlic, thyme, and anchovies to make a smooth paste.

Add the wine and Vegetable Stock to the skillet. Stir in the garlic and anchovy paste together with the sugar.

Bring the mixture to a boil, reduce the heat, cover, and simmer for 30–40 minutes or until the lamb is tender. For the last 10 minutes of the cooking time, remove the lid to allow the sauce to reduce slightly.

Stir the olives into the sauce and mix to combine.

Transfer the lamb and the sauce to a serving bowl and garnish. Serve with creamed potatoes.

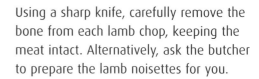

serves 4 | prep 10 mins | cook 35 mins

lamb with bay & lemon

These lamb chops quickly become more elegant when the bone is removed to make noisettes.

INGREDIENTS
4 lamb chops
1 tbsp oil
1 tbsp butter
⅔ cup white wine
⅔ cup Vegetable Stock (see page 29)
2 bay leaves
pared rind of 1 lemon
salt and pepper

Using a sharp knife, carefully remove the bone from each lamb chop, keeping the meat intact. Alternatively, ask the butcher to prepare the lamb noisettes for you.

Shape the meat into rounds and secure with a length of string.

In a large skillet, heat together the oil and butter until the mixture starts to froth.

Add the lamb noisettes to the skillet and cook for 2–3 minutes on each side or until browned all over.

Remove the skillet from the heat, drain off all of the excess fat and discard.

Return the skillet to the heat. Add the wine, Vegetable Stock, bay leaves, and lemon rind to the skillet and cook for 20–25 minutes or until the lamb is tender. Season the lamb noisettes and sauce to taste with a little salt and pepper.

Transfer to serving plates. Remove the string from each noisette and serve with the sauce.

serves 4 | prep 15 mins | cook 1 hr 30 mins

lamb with olives

This is a very simple dish, and the chili adds a bit of spiciness. It is quick to prepare and makes an ideal supper dish.

INGREDIENTS
2 lb 12 oz/1.25 kg boned leg of lamb
⅓ cup olive oil
2 garlic cloves, crushed
1 onion, sliced
1 small red chili, cored, seeded, and
   chopped finely
¾ cup dry white wine
1 cup pitted black olives
salt
chopped fresh parsley, to garnish

Using a sharp knife, cut the lamb into small cubes, about 1 inch /2.5 cm.

Heat the oil in a skillet and fry the garlic, onion, and chili for 5 minutes.

Add the meat and wine and cook for a further 5 minutes.

Stir in the olives, then transfer the mixture to a casserole. Place in a preheated oven, 350°F/180°C, and cook for 1 hour 20 minutes, or until the meat is tender. Season with salt to taste, and serve garnished with chopped fresh parsley.

serves 4 | prep 25 mins | cook 2 hrs

lamb shanks with roasted onions

Slow-roasted lamb is infused with the flavors of garlic and rosemary and served with sweet red onions and glazed carrot sticks. You won't require anything more except a bottle of fruity red wine.

INGREDIENTS
4 x 12 oz/350 g lamb shanks
6 garlic cloves
2 tbsp virgin olive oil
1 tbsp very finely chopped fresh rosemary
salt and pepper
4 red onions
12 oz/350 g carrots, cut into thin sticks
4 tbsp water

Trim off any excess fat from the lamb. Using a small, sharp knife, make 6 incisions in each shank. Cut the garlic cloves lengthwise into 4 slices. Insert 6 garlic slices in the incisions in each lamb shank.

Place the lamb in a single layer in a roasting pan, drizzle with the olive oil, sprinkle with the rosemary, and season with pepper. Roast in a preheated oven, 350°F/180°C, for 45 minutes.

Wrap each of the onions in a square of foil. Remove the roasting pan from the oven and season the lamb shanks with salt. Return the pan to the oven and place the onions on the shelf next to it. Roast for an additional 1–1¼ hours, until the lamb is very tender.

Meanwhile, bring a large pan of water to a boil. Add the carrot sticks and blanch for 1 minute. Drain and refresh under cold water.

Remove the roasting pan from the oven when the lamb is meltingly tender and transfer it to a warmed serving dish. Skim off any fat from the roasting pan and place it over medium heat. Add the carrots and cook for 2 minutes, then add the water, bring to a boil, and let simmer, stirring constantly and scraping up the glazed bits from the bottom of the roasting pan.

Transfer the carrots and sauce to the serving dish. Remove the onions from the oven and unwrap. Cut off and discard about ½ inch/1 cm of the tops and add the onions to the dish. Serve immediately.

serves 4 | prep 35 mins | cook 3 hrs

pot-roasted leg of lamb

This dish from Abruzzo uses a slow cooking method which ensures that the meat absorbs the flavorings and becomes very tender.

INGREDIENTS
3½ lb/1.75 kg leg of lamb
3–4 sprigs fresh rosemary
4½ oz/125 g streaky bacon strips
4 tbsp olive oil
2–3 garlic cloves, crushed
2 onions, sliced
2 carrots, sliced
2 celery stalks, sliced
1¼ cups dry white wine
1 tbsp tomato paste
1¼ cups Vegetable Stock (see page 29)
12 oz/350 g tomatoes, peeled, cut into
   fourths, and seeded
1 tbsp chopped fresh parsley
1 tbsp chopped fresh oregano or marjoram
salt and pepper
fresh rosemary sprigs, to garnish

Wipe the joint of lamb all over, trimming off any excess fat, then season well with salt and pepper, rubbing well in. Lay the sprigs of rosemary over the lamb, cover evenly with the bacon strips, and tie in place with string.

Heat the oil in a skillet and fry the lamb for about 10 minutes or until browned all over, turning several times. Remove the lamb from the skillet.

Transfer the oil from the skillet to a large flameproof casserole and fry the garlic and onion together for 3–4 minutes until they are beginning to soften. Add the carrots and celery and continue to cook for a few minutes longer.

Lay the lamb on top of the vegetables and press down to partly submerge. Pour the wine over the lamb, add the tomato paste, and simmer for 3–4 minutes. Add the stock, tomatoes, herbs, and seasoning and bring back to a boil for a further 3–4 minutes.

Cover the casserole tightly and cook in a moderate oven, 350°F/180°C, for 2–2½ hours until very tender.

Remove the lamb from the casserole and, if preferred, take off the bacon and herbs along with the string. Keep warm. Strain the juices, skimming off any excess fat, and serve in a pitcher. The vegetables may be put around the joint or in a serving dish. Garnish with rosemary sprigs.

serves 4 | prep 20 mins + 30 mins chilling | cook 10 mins

saltimbocca

Originally from Brescia, but now a Roman specialty, saltimbocca literally means «jump in the mouth,» a reflection of just how highly regarded this dish is.

INGREDIENTS
4 veal scallops
2 tbsp lemon juice
salt and pepper
1 tbsp chopped fresh sage leaves
4 slices prosciutto
2 oz/55 g unsalted butter
3 tbsp dry white wine

Place the veal scallops between 2 sheets of plastic wrap and pound with the flat end of a meat mallet or the side of a rolling pin until very thin. Transfer the scallops to a plate and sprinkle with the lemon juice. Set aside for 30 minutes, spooning the juice over them occasionally.

Pat the scallops dry with paper towels, season with salt and pepper, and rub with half the sage. Place a slice of prosciutto on each scallop and secure with a toothpick.

Melt the butter in a large, heavy-bottom skillet. Add the remaining sage and cook over low heat, stirring constantly, for 1 minute. Add the scallops and cook for 3–4 minutes on each side, until golden brown. Pour in the wine and cook for an additional 2 minutes.

Transfer the scallops to a warmed serving dish and pour the pan juices over them. Remove and discard the toothpicks and serve immediately.

COOK'S' TIP
Serve the scallops with fresh lemon wedges to enhance the delicate flavor of the veal.

serves 4 | prep 25 mins | cook 1 hr 35 mins

vitello tonnato

This cold classic, which needs to be prepared the day before you serve it, combines two favorite Italian ingredients—veal and tuna. If you can only find a ready-rolled loin, you will need to unroll the meat before marinating it.

INGREDIENTS
1 lb 10 oz/750 g loin of veal, boned
2 carrots, sliced thinly
1 onion, sliced thinly
2 celery stalks, sliced thinly
2 cloves
2 bay leaves
4 cups dry white wine
salt and pepper
5 oz/140 g canned tuna, drained
4 anchovy fillets, drained and chopped finely
½ cup capers, rinsed and chopped finely
2 oz/55 g gherkins, drained and chopped finely
2 egg yolks
4 tbsp lemon juice
½ cup extra virgin olive oil

to garnish
lemon slices
fresh flat-leaf parsley, chopped finely

Place the veal in a large, nonmetallic dish and add the carrots, onion, celery, cloves, and bay leaves. Pour in the wine and turn the veal to coat. Cover with plastic wrap and put in the refrigerator to marinate overnight.

Drain the veal, reserving the marinade, and roll the meat before wrapping it in a piece of cheesecloth, tying it with string so that it holds its shape. Place the veal in a large pan. Pour the marinade into another pan and bring to a boil. Pour it over the veal and add enough boiling water to cover. Season with salt and pepper, bring back to a boil, then reduce the heat, cover, and let simmer for 1½ hours, until tender but still firm.

Transfer the veal to a plate and set aside to cool completely, then let chill until ready to serve. Strain the cooking liquid into a bowl and set aside to cool.

Combine the tuna, anchovies, capers, and gherkins in a bowl or process in a food processor or blender to make a purée. Beat the egg yolks with the lemon juice in another bowl. Gradually beat in the olive oil, adding it drop by drop to start with and then in a steady stream. When all the oil has been incorporated, stir in the tuna mixture and about 2 tablespoons of the cooled cooking liquid to give the consistency of heavy cream. Season to taste with salt and pepper. Cover with plastic wrap and put in the refrigerator until required.

To serve, unwrap the veal and pat it dry with paper towels. Using a sharp knife, cut the meat into ⅛–¼-inch/3–5-mm thick slices and arrange them on a serving platter. Stir the tuna sauce and spoon it over the veal. Garnish with lemon slices and parsley and serve.

serves 4 | prep 15 mins | cook 1 hr 20 mins

osso bucco

This rich stew of veal, onions, and leeks is Milan's signature dish. It is traditionally served with the saffron-flavored risotto known as risotto alla Milanese.

INGREDIENTS
1 tbsp virgin olive oil
4 tbsp butter
2 onions, chopped
1 leek, chopped
3 tbsp all-purpose flour
salt and pepper
4 thick slices of veal shin (osso bucco)
1¼ cups white wine
1¼ cups Chicken Stock (see page 29)

for the gremolata
2 tbsp chopped fresh parsley
1 garlic clove, chopped finely
grated rind of 1 lemon

Heat the oil and butter in a large, heavy-bottom skillet. Add the onions and leek and cook over low heat, stirring occasionally, for 5 minutes, until softened.

Spread out the flour on a plate and season with salt and pepper. Toss the pieces of veal in the flour to coat, shaking off any excess. Add the veal to the skillet, increase the heat to high and cook until browned on both sides.

Gradually stir in the wine and stock and bring just to a boil, stirring constantly. Reduce the heat, cover, and let simmer for 1¼ hours, or until the veal is very tender.

Meanwhile, make the gremolata by mixing the parsley, garlic, and lemon rind in a small bowl.

Transfer the veal to a warmed serving dish with a slotted spoon. Bring the sauce to a boil and cook, stirring occasionally, until thickened and reduced. Pour the sauce over the veal, sprinkle with the gremolata, and serve immediately.

VARIATION
Modern versions of this dish often include tomatoes. If you like, add 14 oz/400 g canned tomatoes with the wine and stock. You could also add 1 finely chopped carrot and 1 finely chopped celery stalk with the onions and leek.

serves 4 | prep 15 mins | cook 35 mins

sausage & bean casserole

In this traditional Tuscan dish, Italian sausages are cooked with cannellini beans and tomatoes.

INGREDIENTS
8 Italian sausages
1 tbsp olive oil
1 large onion, chopped
2 garlic cloves, chopped
1 green bell pepper
8 oz/225g fresh tomatoes, peeled (see Cook's Tip, page 111) and chopped or 14 oz/400 g canned tomatoes, chopped
2 tbsp sun-dried tomato paste
14 oz/400 g canned cannellini beans
creamed potato or rice, to serve

Using a sharp knife, seed the bell pepper and cut it into thin strips.

Prick the Italian sausages all over with a fork. Cook the sausages, under a preheated broiler, for 10–12 minutes, turning occasionally, until brown all over. Set the sausages aside and keep warm.

Heat the oil in a large skillet. Add the onion, garlic, and bell pepper to the skillet and cook for 5 minutes, stirring occasionally, or until softened.

Add the tomatoes to the skillet and leave the mixture to simmer for about 5 minutes, stirring occasionally, or until slightly reduced and thickened.

Stir the sun-dried tomato paste, cannellini beans, and Italian sausages into the mixture in the skillet. Cook for 4–5 minutes or until the mixture is piping hot. If the mixture becomes too dry during cooking, add 4–5 tablespoons of water.

Transfer the casserole to serving plates and serve with creamed potato or cooked rice.

serves 4 | prep 30 mins | cook 45 mins

prosciutto-wrapped chicken

*Stuffed with ricotta, nutmeg, and spinach,
the chicken breasts are then wrapped with
wafer thin slices of prosciutto di Parma
and gently cooked in white wine.*

INGREDIENTS
½ cup frozen spinach, defrosted
½ cup ricotta cheese
pinch of grated nutmeg
4 skinless, boneless chicken breasts,
  each weighing 6 oz/175 g
4 prosciutto di Parma slices
2 tbsp butter
1 tbsp olive oil
12 small onions or shallots
1½ cups white
  mushrooms, sliced
1 tbsp all-purpose flour
⅔ cup dry white or red wine
1¼ cups Chicken Stock
  (see page 29)
salt and pepper

Put the spinach into a strainer and press out the water with
a spoon. Mix with the ricotta and nutmeg and season with salt
and pepper to taste.

Using a sharp knife, slit each chicken breast through the side and
enlarge each cut to form a pocket. Fill with the spinach mixture,
reshape the chicken breasts, wrap each breast tightly in a slice of
prosciutto, and secure with a toothpick. Cover the chicken and chill
in the refrigerator.

Heat the butter and oil in a skillet and brown the chicken breasts
for 2 minutes on each side. Transfer the chicken to a large, shallow
heatproof dish and keep warm until required.

Fry the onions and mushrooms for 2–3 minutes until lightly
browned. Stir in the flour, then gradually add the wine and stock.
Bring to a boil, stirring constantly. Season with salt and pepper and
spoon the mixture around the chicken.

Cook the chicken uncovered in a preheated oven, 400°F/200°C, for
20 minutes. Turn the breasts over and cook for a further 10 minutes.
Remove the toothpicks and serve with the sauce, together with
carrot purée and green beans, if wished.

serves 6 | prep 35 mins | cook 2 hrs

italian-style roast

A mixture of cheese, rosemary, and sun-dried tomatoes is stuffed under the chicken skin, then roasted with garlic, potatoes, and vegetables.

INGREDIENTS
5 lb 8 oz/2.5 kg chicken
sprigs of fresh rosemary
¾ cup feta cheese, grated coarsely
2 tbsp sun-dried tomato paste
4 tbsp butter, softened
1 bulb garlic
2 lb 4 oz/1 kg new potatoes, halved if large
1 each red, green, and yellow bell pepper, cut into chunks
3 zucchinis, sliced thinly
2 tbsp olive oil
2 tbsp all-purpose flour
2½ cups Chicken Stock (see page 29)
salt and pepper

Rinse the chicken inside and out with cold water and drain well. Carefully cut between the skin and the top of the breast meat using a small pointed knife. Slide a finger into the slit and carefully enlarge it to form a pocket. Continue until the skin is completely lifted away from both breasts and the top of the legs.

Chop the leaves from 3 rosemary stems. Mix with the feta cheese, sun-dried tomato paste, butter, and pepper to taste, then spoon under the skin. Put the chicken in a large roasting pan, cover with foil, and cook in a preheated oven, 375°F/190°C, for 20 minutes per 1 lb 2 oz/500 g, plus 20 minutes.

Break the garlic bulb into cloves but do not peel. Add the vegetables to the chicken after 40 minutes.

Drizzle with oil, tuck in a few stems of rosemary, and season with salt and pepper. Cook for the remaining calculated time, removing the foil for the last 40 minutes to brown the chicken.

Transfer the chicken to a serving platter. Place some of the vegetables around the chicken and transfer the remainder to a warmed serving dish. Pour the fat out of the roasting pan and stir the flour into the remaining pan juices. Cook for 2 minutes then gradually stir in the stock. Bring to a boil, stirring until thickened. Strain into a gravy boat and serve with the chicken.

serves 4 | prep 15 mins | cook 1 hr 30 mins

chicken with green olives

Olives are a popular flavoring for poultry and game in the Apulia region, where this recipe originates.

INGREDIENTS
3 tbsp olive oil
2 tbsp butter
4 chicken breasts, part boned
1 large onion, chopped finely
2 garlic cloves, crushed
2 red, yellow, or green bell peppers, cored, seeded, and cut into large pieces
9 oz/250 g white mushrooms, sliced or cut into fourths
6 oz/175 g tomatoes, skinned and halved
⅔ cup dry white wine
1½ cups pitted green olives
4–6 tbsp heavy cream
14 oz/400 g dried pasta
salt and pepper
chopped fresh flat-leaf parsley, to garnish

Heat 2 tbsp of the oil and the butter in a skillet. Add the chicken breasts and fry until golden brown all over. Remove the chicken from the skillet.

Add the onion and garlic to the skillet and fry over medium heat until beginning to soften. Add the bell peppers and mushrooms and cook for 2–3 minutes.

Add the tomatoes and season to taste with salt and pepper. Transfer the vegetables to a casserole and arrange the chicken on top.

Add the wine to the skillet and bring to a boil. Pour the wine over the chicken. Cover and cook in a preheated oven at 350°F/180°C for 50 minutes.

Add the olives to the casserole and mix in. Pour in the cream, cover, and return to the oven for 10–20 minutes.

Meanwhile, bring a large pan of lightly salted water to a boil. Add the pasta and the remaining oil and cook for 8–10 minutes or until tender, but still firm to the bite. Drain the pasta well and transfer to a serving dish.

Arrange the chicken on top of the pasta, spoon over the sauce, garnish with the parsley, and serve immediately. Alternatively, place the pasta in a large serving bowl and serve separately.

serves 4 | prep 15 mins | cook 40 mins

chicken peperonata

All the sunshine colors and flavors of Italy are combined in this easy dish.

INGREDIENTS
8 chicken thighs
2 tbsp whole wheat flour
2 tbsp olive oil
1 small onion, sliced thinly
1 garlic clove, crushed
1 each large red, yellow, and green bell
   peppers, sliced thinly
14 oz/400 g canned chopped tomatoes
1 tbsp chopped oregano
salt and pepper
fresh oregano, to garnish
crusty whole wheat bread,
   to serve

Remove the skin from the chicken thighs and toss them in the flour.

Heat the oil in a wide skillet and fry the chicken quickly until sealed and lightly browned, then remove from the skillet.

Add the onion to the skillet and fry until soft. Add the garlic, bell peppers, tomatoes, and oregano, then bring to a boil, stirring.

Arrange the chicken over the vegetables, season well with salt and pepper, then cover the skillet tightly and simmer for 20–25 minutes or until the chicken is completely cooked and tender.

Season with salt and pepper to taste, garnish with oregano, and serve with crusty whole wheat bread.

COOK'S TIP
For extra flavor, halve the bell peppers and broil under a preheated broiler until the skins are charred. Leave to cool then remove the skins and seeds. Slice the bell peppers thinly and use them in the recipe.

serves 4 | prep 25 mins | cook 20 mins

chicken with smoked ham & parmesan

There is much more to the cuisine of Bologna than the eponymous pasta dish, as it is renowned for its rich dishes. The capital of the Emilia-Romagna region, Bologna is nicknamed la grassa—the fat, rich, and plentiful one.

INGREDIENTS
4 skinned, boned chicken breasts
2 tbsp all-purpose flour
salt and pepper
2 oz/55 g unsalted butter
8 thin slices smoked ham, trimmed
2 oz/55 g freshly grated Parmesan cheese
fresh basil sprigs, to garnish

Cut each chicken breast through the thickness to open them out, then place the pieces between 2 sheets of plastic wrap and pound with the flat end of a meat mallet or the side of a rolling pin until they are as thin as possible. Spread out the flour on a shallow plate and season with salt and pepper. Coat the chicken pieces in the seasoned flour, shaking off any excess.

Melt half the butter in a large, heavy-bottom skillet. Add the chicken pieces, in batches if necessary, and cook over medium heat, turning frequently, for 10–15 minutes, until they are golden brown all over and cooked through.

Meanwhile, melt the remaining butter in a small pan. Remove the skillet containing the chicken from the heat. Place a slice of ham on each piece of chicken and sprinkle with the cheese. Pour the melted butter over the chicken and return the skillet to the heat for 3–4 minutes, until the cheese has melted. Serve immediately, garnished with basil sprigs.

VARIATION
A similar dish is made in the Valle d'Aosta, but instead of the chicken breasts being cut and opened out, they are slit to make a pocket. The pockets are then filled with slices of smoked ham or prosciutto and fontina cheese before cooking.

serves 4 | prep 10 mins | cook 35 mins

chicken & balsamic vinegar

A rich caramelized sauce, flavored with balsamic vinegar and wine, adds a piquant flavor. The chicken needs to be marinated overnight.

INGREDIENTS
4 chicken thighs, boned
2 garlic cloves, crushed
¾ cup red wine
3 tbsp white wine vinegar
1 tbsp oil
1 tbsp butter
6 shallots
3 tbsp balsamic vinegar
2 tbsp fresh thyme
salt and pepper
cooked polenta or rice, to serve

Using a sharp knife, make a few slashes in the chicken skin. Brush the chicken with the crushed garlic and place in a non-metallic dish.

Pour the wine and white wine vinegar over the chicken and season with salt and pepper to taste. Cover and leave to marinate in the refrigerator overnight.

Remove the chicken pieces with a slotted spoon, draining well, and reserve the marinade.

Heat the oil and butter in a skillet. Add the shallots and cook for 2–3 minutes or until they begin to soften.

Add the chicken pieces to the skillet and cook for 3-4 minutes, turning, until browned all over. Reduce the heat and add half of the reserved marinade. Cover and cook for 15–20 minutes, adding more marinade when necessary.

Once the chicken is tender, add the balsamic vinegar and thyme and cook for a further 4 minutes.

Transfer the chicken and marinade to serving plates and serve with polenta or rice.

serves 4 | prep 30 mins | cook 3 hrs 30 mins

lombardy duck

Rich meat, such as duck and goose, is combined with lentils in the cuisines of many countries and Italy is no exception. This is a wonderfully flavorsome dish that would be a good choice when entertaining as it can be prepared in advance and gently reheated.

INGREDIENTS
for the stock
1 celery stalk
1 garlic clove
6 peppercorns, crushed lightly
1 bay leaf
5 sprigs fresh flat-leaf parsley
1 onion
1 clove
salt

5 lb/2.25 kg duck
1⅓ cups small brown lentils, rinsed
1 tbsp virgin olive oil
2 onions
2 celery stalks
2 tbsp brandy or grappa
⅔ cup dry white wine
salt and pepper
1 tsp cornstarch

Cut the duck into joints. Cut off the wings. Fold back the skin at the neck end and cut out the wishbone with a small, sharp knife. Using poultry shears or heavy kitchen scissors, cut the duck breast in half along the breastbone, from the tail end to the neck. Cut along each side of the backbone to separate the 2 halves. Remove the backbone. Cut each portion in half diagonally.

To make the stock, place the wings and backbone in a large pan and add the celery, garlic, peppercorns, bay leaf, and parsley. Stick the onion with the clove and add to the pan with a large pinch of salt. Add cold water to cover and bring to a boil. Skim off any scum that rises to the surface. Then reduce the heat and let simmer very gently for 2 hours. Strain into a clean pan and boil until reduced and concentrated. Measure ⅔ cup and set aside all the stock.

Place the lentils in a pan with enough cold water to cover. Add the olive oil. Cut 1 onion in half and add with 1 celery stalk. Bring to a boil over medium heat, reduce the heat and let simmer for 15 minutes, until the lentils are starting to soften. Drain and set aside.

Meanwhile, put the duck portions, skin-side down, in a heavy-bottom skillet and cook, shaking the skillet occasionally, for about 10 minutes. Transfer the duck portions to a flameproof casserole and drain off the excess fat from the skillet. Finely chop the remaining onion and celery and add to the skillet. Cook over low heat, stirring occasionally, for 5 minutes, until softened. Using a slotted spoon, transfer the vegetables to the casserole.

Set the casserole over medium heat, add the brandy, and ignite. When the flames have died down, add the wine and the reserved measured stock. Bring to a boil, add the lentils, and season with salt and pepper. Cover and simmer over low heat for 40 minutes.

Combine the cornstarch with 2 tablespoons of the stock to a smooth paste in a small bowl. Stir the paste into the casserole and cook, stirring frequently, for about 5 minutes, until thickened. Taste and adjust the seasoning, if necessary, and serve immediately.

serves 4 | prep 15 mins | cook 40 mins

pesto baked partridge

Partridge has a more delicate flavor than many game birds and this subtle sauce perfectly complements it.

INGREDIENTS
8 partridge pieces (about 4 oz/115 g each)
4 tbsp butter, melted
4 tbsp Dijon mustard
2 tbsp lime juice
1 tbsp brown sugar
6 tbsp Green Pesto Sauce (see page 28)
1 lb/450 g dried rigatoni
1 tbsp olive oil
1⅓ cups freshly grated Parmesan cheese
salt and pepper

Arrange the partridge pieces, smooth side down, in a single layer in a large, ovenproof dish.

Mix together the butter, Dijon mustard, lime juice, and brown sugar in a bowl. Season to taste. Brush this mixture over the partridge pieces and bake in a preheated oven at 400°F/200°C for 15 minutes.

Remove the dish from the oven and coat the partridge pieces with 3 tablespoons of the Green Pesto Sauce. Return to the oven and bake for a further 12 minutes.

Remove the dish from the oven and carefully turn over the partridge pieces. Coat the top of the partridge pieces with the remaining mustard mixture and return to the oven for a further 10 minutes.

Meanwhile, bring a large pan of lightly salted water to a boil. Add the rigatoni and olive oil and cook for 8–10 minutes until tender, but still firm to the bite. Drain and transfer to a serving dish and toss with the remaining Green Pesto Sauce and the Parmesan cheese.

Serve the partridge with the pasta, pouring over the cooking juices.

VARIATION
You could also prepare young pheasant in the same way.

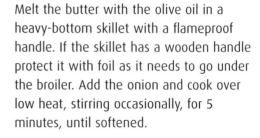

serves 3 | prep 10 mins | cook 30 mins

seafood omelet

This substantial omelet makes a quick and easy mid-week supper dish—a nourishing main course for a family meal. For a larger family, double the quantity and use 2 skillets.

INGREDIENTS
2 tbsp unsalted butter
1 tbsp olive oil
1 onion, chopped very finely
6 oz/175 g zucchinis, halved lengthwise
    and sliced
1 celery stalk, chopped very finely
3 oz/85 g white mushrooms, sliced
2 oz/55 g green beans, cut into
    2-inch/5-cm lengths
4 eggs
⅜ cup mascarpone cheese
1 tbsp chopped fresh thyme
1 tbsp shredded fresh basil
salt and pepper
7 oz/200 g canned tuna, drained and flaked
4 oz/115 g shelled cooked shrimp

Melt the butter with the olive oil in a heavy-bottom skillet with a flameproof handle. If the skillet has a wooden handle protect it with foil as it needs to go under the broiler. Add the onion and cook over low heat, stirring occasionally, for 5 minutes, until softened.

Add the zucchinis, celery, mushrooms, and beans and cook, stirring occasionally, for an additional 8–10 minutes, until the mixture is starting to brown.

Beat the eggs with the mascarpone, thyme, basil, and salt and pepper to taste.

Add the tuna to the skillet and stir it into the mixture with a wooden spoon. Add the shrimp last.

Pour the egg mixture into the skillet and cook for 5 minutes, until it is just starting to set. Draw the egg from the sides of the skillet toward the center to let the uncooked egg run underneath.

Put the skillet under a preheated broiler and cook until the egg is just set and the surface is starting to brown. Cut the omelet into wedges and serve.

serves 4 | prep 20 mins + 30 mins resting | cook 30 mins

deep-fried seafood

Like many seafood recipes, this popular dish comes from the Campania region of southern Italy. It invariably contains a mixture of white fish fillets and shellfish, but the precise ingredients will depend on the day's catch.

INGREDIENTS
for the batter
¾ cup all-purpose flour
salt
1 egg yolk
1 tbsp olive oil
1 cup milk
2 egg whites

corn oil, for frying
7 oz/200 g white fish fillets, such as lemon sole, skinned and cut into strips
7 oz/200 g angler fish fillets, cut into bite-size chunks
4 shelled scallops, with or without corals
8 oz/225 g large cooked shrimp, shelled but with the tails intact

to garnish
fresh flat-leaf parsley sprigs
lemon wedges

First, make the batter. Sift the flour with a pinch of salt into a bowl and make a well in the center. Add the egg yolk and olive oil to the well and mix together with a wooden spoon, gradually incorporating the flour. Gradually beat in the milk to make a smooth batter. Cover and set aside to rest for 30 minutes.

Heat the corn oil in a deep-fryer to 350–375°F/180–190°C or, if using a heavy-bottom skillet, until a cube of day-old bread browns in 30 seconds.

Meanwhile, whisk the egg whites in another bowl until they form stiff peaks, then gently fold them into the batter.

Using tongs, dip the fish and shellfish, a piece at a time, into the batter to coat, then add to the skillet and cook for 3–4 minutes, until crisp and golden. Do not overcrowd the skillet. As each piece is cooked, remove it from the skillet and drain on paper towels. Transfer to a serving platter and keep it warm while you cook the remaining fish and shellfish. Garnish with parsley sprigs and lemon wedges and serve.

serves 4 | prep 25 mins | cook 30 mins

roast sea bream with fennel

All sea bream—and it is quite a large family of fish—is delicately flavored and especially delicious when stuffed and roasted. If possible, try to obtain gilt head sea bream, known as orata in Italy, for this recipe.

INGREDIENTS
2¼ cups dried, uncolored bread crumbs
2 tbsp milk
1 fennel bulb, sliced thinly, fronds reserved
   for garnish
1 tbsp lemon juice
2 tbsp Sambuca*
1 tbsp chopped fresh thyme
1 bay leaf, crumbled
3 lb 5 oz/1.5 kg whole sea bream, cleaned,
   scaled, and boned
salt and pepper
3 tbsp olive oil, plus extra for brushing
1 red onion, chopped
1¼ cups dry white wine

Place the bread crumbs in a bowl, add the milk, and set aside for 5 minutes to soak. Place the fennel in another bowl and add the lemon juice, Sambuca, thyme, and bay leaf. Squeeze the bread crumbs and add them to the mixture, stirring well.

Rinse the fish inside and out under cold running water and pat dry with paper towels. Season with salt and pepper. Spoon the fennel mixture into the cavity, then bind the fish with trussing thread or kitchen string.

Brush a large ovenproof dish with olive oil and sprinkle the onion over the bottom. Lay the fish on top and pour in the wine—it should reach about one-third of the way up the fish. Drizzle the sea bream with the olive oil and cook in a preheated oven, 475°F/240°C, for 25–30 minutes. Baste the fish occasionally with the cooking juices and if it starts to brown, cover it with a piece of foil to protect it.

Carefully lift out the fish, remove the string, and place on a warmed serving platter. Garnish with the reserved fennel fronds and serve immediately.

COOK'S TIP
Sambuca is an Italian liqueur distilled from witch elder, but it has a strong aniseed flavor, which marries well with fish. If it is unavailable, substitute Pernod.

serves 4 | prep 15 mins | cook 35 mins

swordfish with olives & capers

Swordfish is plentiful in the waters surrounding Sicily, where it is usually cooked with traditional Mediterranean ingredients. This recipe comes from Palermo, Sicily's main port.

INGREDIENTS
2 tbsp all-purpose flour
salt and pepper
4 x 8 oz/225 g swordfish steaks
generous ⅓ cup olive oil
2 garlic cloves, halved
1 onion, chopped
4 anchovy fillets, drained and chopped
4 tomatoes, peeled (see Cook's Tip, page 111), seeded, and chopped
12 green olives, pitted and sliced
1 tbsp capers, rinsed
fresh rosemary leaves, to garnish

Spread out the flour on a plate and season with salt and pepper. Coat the fish in the seasoned flour, shaking off any excess.

Gently heat the olive oil in a large, heavy-bottom skillet. Add the garlic and cook over low heat for 2–3 minutes, until just golden. Do not let it turn brown or burn. Remove the garlic and discard.

Add the fish to the skillet and cook over medium heat for about 4 minutes on each side, until cooked through and golden brown. Remove the steaks from the skillet and set aside.

Add the onion and anchovies to the skillet and cook, mashing the anchovies with a wooden spoon until they have turned to a purée and the onion is golden. Add the tomatoes and cook over low heat, stirring occasionally, for about 20 minutes, until the mixture has thickened.

Stir in the olives and capers and taste and adjust the seasoning. Return the steaks to the skillet and heat through gently. Serve garnished with rosemary.

serves 8 | prep 1 hr 15 mins | cook 1 hr 30 mins

sole fillets in marsala

A rich wine and cream sauce makes this an excellent dinner party dish. Make the stock the day before to cut down on the preparation time.

INGREDIENTS
1 tbsp peppercorns, crushed lightly
8 sole fillets
⅓ cup Marsala
⅔ cup heavy cream

for the stock
2½ cups water
bones and skin from the sole fillets
1 onion, peeled and halved
1 carrot, peeled and halved
3 fresh bay leaves

for the sauce
1 tbsp olive oil
1 tbsp butter
4 shallots, chopped finely
3½ oz/100 g baby white mushrooms,
   wiped and halved

To make the stock, place the water, fish bones and skin, onion, carrot, and bay leaves in a large pan and bring to a boil.

Reduce the heat and leave the mixture to simmer for 1 hour or until the stock has reduced to about ⅔ cup. Drain the stock through a fine strainer, discarding the bones and vegetables, and set aside.

To make the sauce, heat the oil and butter in a skillet. Add the shallots and cook, stirring, for 2–3 minutes or until just softened.

Add the mushrooms to the skillet and cook, stirring, for a further 2–3 minutes or until they are just beginning to brown.

Add the peppercorns and sole fillets to the skillet in batches. Fry the sole fillets for 3–4 minutes on each side or until golden brown. Remove the fish with a slotted spoon, then set aside and keep warm while you cook the remainder.

When all the fillets have been cooked and removed from the skillet, pour the wine and stock into the skillet and leave to simmer for 3 minutes. Increase the heat and boil the mixture in the skillet for about 5 minutes or until the sauce has reduced and thickened.

Pour in the cream and heat through. Pour the sauce over the fish and serve with the cooked vegetables of your choice.

serves 4 | prep 15 mins | cook 40 mins

italian cod

A delicious spiced crunchy topping infuses the fish with flavor during cooking and prevents it from losing moisture.

INGREDIENTS
2 tbsp butter
⅞ cup fresh whole wheat bread crumbs
1 heaping tbsp chopped walnuts
grated rind and juice of 2 lemons
2 fresh rosemary sprigs, stalks removed
2 tbsp chopped fresh parsley
4 cod fillets, about
    5½ oz/150 g each
1 garlic clove, crushed
1 small fresh red chili, diced
3 tbsp walnut oil
mixed salad greens, to serve

Preheat the oven to 400°F/200°C. Melt the butter in a large pan over low heat, stirring constantly. Remove the pan from the heat and add the bread crumbs, walnuts, the rind and juice of 1 lemon, half the rosemary, and half the parsley, stirring until mixed.

Press the bread crumb mixture over the top of the cod fillets. Place the cod fillets in a shallow foil-lined roasting pan. Roast the fish in the oven for 25–30 minutes.

Mix the garlic, the remaining lemon rind and juice, rosemary, parsley, and the chili together in a bowl. Beat in the oil and mix to combine. Drizzle the dressing over the cod steaks as soon as they are cooked. Transfer the fish to warmed serving plates and serve at once with salad greens.

VARIATION
If preferred, the walnuts may be omitted from the crust. In addition, extra virgin olive oil can be used instead of walnut oil, if you like.

serves 4 | prep 15 mins + 30 mins marinating | cook 15 mins

sicilian tuna

This quick, spicy dish can be cooked in the kitchen or outdoors on the grill. It needs nothing more than a crisp green salad as an accompaniment.

INGREDIENTS
for the marinade
½ **cup extra virgin olive oil**
4 garlic cloves, chopped finely
4 fresh red chilies, seeded and
  chopped finely
juice and finely grated rind of 2 lemons
4 tbsp finely chopped fresh flat-leaf parsley
salt and pepper

4 x 5 oz/140 g tuna steaks
2 fennel bulbs, sliced thickly lengthwise
2 red onions, sliced
2 tbsp virgin olive oil
crusty rolls, to serve

First, make the marinade, by whisking all the ingredients together in a bowl. Place the tuna steaks in a large shallow dish and spoon over 4 tablespoons of the marinade, turning to coat. Cover and set aside for 30 minutes. Set aside the remaining marinade.

Heat a ridged grill pan. Put the fennel and onions in a bowl, add the oil, and toss well to coat. Add to the grill pan and cook for 5 minutes on each side, until just starting to color. Transfer to warmed serving plates, drizzle with the reserved marinade and keep warm.

Add the tuna steaks to the grill pan and cook, turning once, for 4–5 minutes, until firm to the touch, but still moist inside. Transfer the tuna to the plates and serve immediately with crusty rolls.

serves 4 | prep 20 mins | cook 45 mins

stuffed squid

Squid can be tricky to cook properly. To avoid making it tough, it should either be cooked very quickly or stewed slowly on a very low heat in the Italian way.

INGREDIENTS
8 sun-dried tomatoes
8 small prepared squid (bodies about
   5 inches/13 cm long)
1½ cups fresh white bread crumbs
2 tbsp capers, rinsed and chopped finely
2 tbsp chopped fresh flat-leaf parsley
salt and pepper
1 egg white
olive oil, for brushing and drizzling
3 tbsp dry white wine
lemon juice, for drizzling (optional)

Put the sun-dried tomatoes in a bowl and cover with boiling water. Set aside for 15–20 minutes.

Meanwhile, finely chop the squid tentacles and place in another bowl. Add the bread crumbs, capers, and parsley.

Thoroughly drain the tomatoes and pat dry with paper towels. Chop them finely and add to the bread crumb mixture. Mix thoroughly and season to taste with salt and pepper. Stir in the egg white.

Spoon the bread crumb mixture into the squid body sacs, pushing it down well. Do not fill them more than about three-quarters full or they will burst during cooking. Secure the opening of each sac with a toothpick so the stuffing will not ooze out.

Generously brush oil over a heatproof dish large enough to hold the squid snugly in a single layer. Place the squid in the dish and pour in the wine. Cover with foil and bake in a preheated oven, 325°F/160°C, for about 45 minutes, turning and basting occasionally. Test with a fork to check if the squid is tender.

Remove from the oven and set aside to cool to room temperature. To serve, remove and discard the toothpicks and slice the squid into circles. Place on warmed individual plates and drizzle with a little olive oil and either the cooled cooking juices or lemon juice.

serves 4 | prep 15 mins | cook 20 mins

vegetable frittata

A frittata is a type of Italian omelet—you can add almost anything to the eggs. It is also delicious eaten cold and makes an ideal picnic dish.

INGREDIENTS
3 tbsp olive oil
1 onion, chopped
2 garlic cloves, chopped
8 oz/225 g zucchinis,
   sliced thinly
4 eggs
14 oz/400 g canned borlotti beans,
   drained and rinsed
3 tomatoes, skinned and chopped
2 tbsp chopped fresh parsley
1 tbsp chopped fresh basil
½ cup grated Swiss cheese
salt and pepper

Heat 2 tablespoons of the oil in a skillet, add the onion and garlic, and fry gently, stirring occasionally, for 2–3 minutes or until soft. Add the zucchinis and cook for 3–4 minutes, or until softened.

Break the eggs into a bowl and add salt and pepper to taste, the fried vegetables, beans, tomatoes, and herbs.

Heat the remaining oil in a 9½-inch/24-cm omelet pan, add the egg mixture, and fry gently for 5 minutes until the eggs have almost set and the underside is brown.

Sprinkle the cheese over the top and place the pan under a preheated moderate broiler for 3–4 minutes or until set on the top but still moist in the middle. Cut into wedges and serve warm or at room temperature.

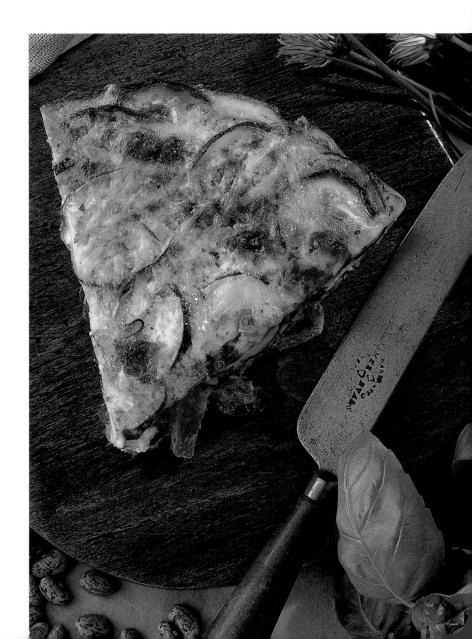

serves 4 | prep 25 mins | cook 50 mins

spinach & ricotta pie

Although this pie looks very impressive it is actually fairly easy to make. It can be served either hot or cold.

INGREDIENTS
8 oz/225 g spinach
1 oz/25 g pine nuts
3½ oz/100 g ricotta cheese
2 large eggs, beaten
1¾ oz/50 g ground almonds
1½ oz/40 g Parmesan cheese, grated
9 oz/250 g pie dough, defrosted if frozen
1 small egg, beaten

Rinse the spinach, place in a large pan and cook for 4–5 minutes until it has wilted. Drain thoroughly. When the spinach is cool enough to handle, squeeze out the excess liquid.

Place the pine nuts on a cookie sheet and lightly toast under a preheated broiler for 2–3 minutes or until golden.

Place the ricotta, spinach, and eggs in a bowl and mix together. Add the pine nuts, beat well, then stir in the ground almonds and Parmesan cheese.

Roll out the puff pastry and make 2 x 8-inch/20-cm squares. Trim the edges, reserving the pastry trimmings.

Place 1 pastry square on a cookie sheet. Spoon over the spinach mixture, keeping within ½ inch/12 mm of the edge of the pastry. Brush the edges with beaten egg and place the second square over the top.

Using a round-bladed knife, press the pastry edges together by tapping along the sealed edge. Use the pastry trimmings to make a few leaves to decorate the pie.

Prick the top of the pie several times with a fork, brush with the beaten egg, and bake in a preheated oven, 425°F/220°C, for 10 minutes. Reduce the oven temperature to 375°F/190°C and bake the pie for a further 25–30 minutes.

serves 8 | prep 30 mins | cook 30 mins

roasted bell pepper terrine

This delicious terrine is an ideal lunch dish. It goes particularly well with Italian bread and a green salad.

INGREDIENTS
3 cups fava beans
6 red bell peppers, halved and seeded
3 small zucchinis, sliced
   lengthwise
1 eggplant, sliced lengthwise
3 leeks, halved lengthwise
6 tbsp olive oil, plus extra for greasing
6 tbsp light cream
2 tbsp chopped fresh basil
salt and pepper

Grease a 5-cup terrine. Blanch the fava beans in boiling water for 1–2 minutes and pop them out of their skins. It is not essential to do this, but the effort is worthwhile as the beans taste a lot sweeter.

Roast the bell peppers over a hot grill until the skin is black—about 10–15 minutes. Remove and put into a plastic bag. Seal and set aside.

Brush the zucchinis, eggplant, and leeks with 5 tablespoons of the olive oil, and season with salt and pepper to taste. Cook over the hot grill until tender, about 8–10 minutes, turning once.

Meanwhile, purée the fava beans in a blender or food processor with 1 tablespoon of the olive oil, the cream, and the seasoning. Alternatively, chop and then press through a strainer.

Remove the bell peppers from the plastic bag and peel by rubbing the skins gently away from the bell peppers.

Put a layer of bell pepper along the bottom and up the sides of the terrine.

Spread a third of the bean purée over the bell pepper. Cover the purée layer with the eggplant slices and spread over half of the remaining bean purée.

Sprinkle over the basil. Top with zucchinis and the remaining bean purée.

Lay the leeks on top of the purée layer. Add any remaining pieces of bell pepper. Put a piece of foil, folded 4 times, on the top and weigh down with cans.

Chill until required. Turn out onto a serving platter, slice, and serve with Italian bread and a green salad.

serves 4 | prep 40 mins | cook 1 hr 5 mins

eggplants with mozzarella & parmesan

This can be served with a salad as a main course and it also makes a delicious accompaniment to plainly cooked chicken, pork, or veal.

INGREDIENTS
3 eggplants, sliced thinly
salt
olive oil, for brushing
10½ oz/300 g mozzarella cheese, sliced
1 cup freshly grated Parmesan cheese
3 tbsp dried, uncolored bread crumbs
1 tbsp butter
fresh flat-leaf parsley sprigs, to garnish

for the tomato and basil sauce
2 tbsp virgin olive oil
4 shallots, chopped finely
2 garlic cloves, chopped finely
14 oz/400 g canned tomatoes
1 tsp sugar
8 fresh basil leaves, shredded
salt and pepper

To remove any bitterness, layer the eggplant slices in a colander, sprinkling each layer with salt. Stand the colander in the sink and let drain for 30 minutes. Rinse thoroughly under cold running water to remove all traces of salt, then pat dry with paper towels.

Arrange the eggplant slices in a single layer on 1–2 large cookie sheets. Brush with olive oil and bake in a preheated oven, 400°F/200°C, for 15–20 minutes, until tender, but not collapsing.

Meanwhile, make the tomato and basil sauce. Heat the oil in a heavy-bottom pan, add the shallots, and cook, stirring occasionally, for 5 minutes, until softened. Add the garlic and cook for 1 minute more. Add the tomatoes, with their can juices, and break them up with a wooden spoon. Stir in the sugar and season to taste with salt and pepper. Bring to a boil, reduce the heat, and let simmer for about 10 minutes, until thickened. Stir in the basil leaves.

Brush a heatproof dish with olive oil and arrange half the eggplant slices in the bottom. Cover with half the mozzarella, spoon over half the tomato sauce, and sprinkle with half the Parmesan. Mix the remaining Parmesan with the bread crumbs. Make more layers, ending with the Parmesan mixture.

Dot the top with butter and bake for 25 minutes, until the topping is golden brown. Remove from the oven and let stand for 5 minutes, before slicing and serving, garnished with parsley.

part four

PANE & PIZZE
bread & pizza

There is an enormous range of different kinds of bread in Italy, made from a variety of ingredients, including yeast, olive oil, sun-dried tomatoes, roasted bell peppers, olives, and herbs. Bread really is a staple of the diet in Italy and is eaten throughout every meal.

Italians were the inventors of the original fast food, the pizza—here you will find just some of the delicious recipes from the almost infinite variety that can be found in Italian pizzerias.

serves 12 | prep 25 mins + 2 hrs rising | cook 35 mins

black olive focaccia

Focaccia is an Italian flatbread made with olive oil. Try serving it with soups or salads, or on its own as an indulgent snack at any time of day.

INGREDIENTS
scant 4 cups white bread flour, plus extra for dusting
1 tsp salt
2 tsp active dry yeast
1½ cups tepid water
6 tbsp extra virgin olive oil, plus extra for brushing
⅔ cup pitted black olives, chopped coarsely
1 tsp rock salt

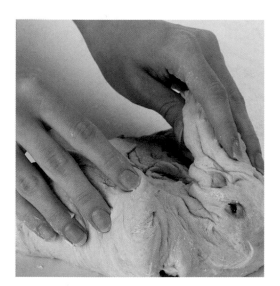

Sift the flour and salt into a warmed bowl and stir in the yeast. Pour in the water and 2 tablespoons of the olive oil and mix to a soft dough. Knead the dough on a lightly floured counter for 5–10 minutes, or until it becomes smooth and elastic. Transfer it to a clean, warmed, oiled bowl and cover with plastic wrap. Let stand in a warm place for 1 hour, or until the dough has doubled in size.

Brush 2 cookie sheets with oil. Punch the dough to knock out the air, then knead on a lightly floured counter for 1 minute. Add the olives and knead until combined. Divide the dough in half and shape into 2 ovals 11 x 9 inches/28 x 23 cm long, and place on the prepared cookie sheets. Cover with oiled plastic wrap and let stand in a warm place for 1 hour, or until the dough is puffy.

Preheat the oven to 400°F/200°C. Press your fingers into the dough to make dimples, drizzle over 2 tablespoons of oil, and sprinkle with the rock salt. Bake in the preheated oven for 30–35 minutes, or until golden. Drizzle with the remaining olive oil and cover with a cloth, to give a soft crust. Slice each loaf into 6 pieces and serve warm.

COOK'S TIP
As the flavor of the olive oil is the most important part of this bread recipe, try to use a good-quality, well-flavored olive oil.

serves 4 | prep 15 mins + 45 mins fermenting/rising | cook 30 mins

olive oil bread with cheese

This flat cheese bread is sometimes called foccacia. It is delicious served with antipasto or simply on its own. This recipe makes one loaf.

INGREDIENTS
½ oz/15 g dried yeast
1 tsp sugar
9 fl oz/250 ml hand-hot water
12 oz/350 g white bread flour
1 tsp salt
3 tbsp olive oil
200 g/7 oz pecorino cheese, cubed
½ tbsp fennel seeds, crushed lightly

COOK'S TIP
Pecorino is a hard, quite salty cheese, which is sold in most large supermarkets and Italian delicatessens. If you cannot obtain pecorino, use sharp Cheddar or Parmesan cheese instead.

Mix the yeast with the sugar and 8 tablespoons of the water. Leave to ferment in a warm place for about 15 minutes.

Mix the flour with the salt. Add 1 tablespoon of the oil, the yeast mixture, and the remaining water to form a smooth dough. Knead the dough for 4 minutes.

Divide the dough into 2 equal portions. Roll out each portion to form a round ¼ inch/6 mm thick. Place 1 round on a cookie sheet.

Scatter the cheese and half of the fennel seeds evenly over the round of dough.

Place the second round on top and squeeze the edges together to seal so that the filling does not leak during the cooking time.

Using a sharp knife, make a few slashes in the top of the dough and brush with the remaining olive oil.

Sprinkle with the remaining fennel seeds and leave the dough to rise for 20–30 minutes.

Bake in a preheated oven, at 400°F/200°C, for 30 minutes or until golden brown. Serve immediately.

serves 4 | prep 15 mins + 45 mins fermenting/rising | cook 35 mins

sun-dried tomato loaf

This delicious tomato bread is great with cheese or soup or for making an unusual sandwich. This recipe makes one loaf.

INGREDIENTS
¼ oz/7 g dried yeast
1 tsp granulated sugar
1¼ cups lukewarm water
1 lb/450 g white bread flour
1 tsp salt
2 tsp dried basil
2 tbsp sun-dried tomato paste
  or tomato paste
margarine, for greasing
12 sun-dried tomatoes in oil, drained
  and cut into strips

Place the yeast and sugar in a bowl and mix with ½ cup of the water. Let the mixture stand in a warm place to ferment for 15 minutes.

Strain the flour and salt into a bowl. Make a well in the center and add the basil, yeast mixture, tomato paste, and half of the remaining water. Using a wooden spoon, draw the flour into the liquid and mix to form a dough, adding the rest of the water gradually.

Turn out onto a floured counter and knead for 5 minutes. Cover with oiled plastic wrap and let stand in a warm place for 30 minutes or until doubled in size.

Lightly grease a 2-lb/900-g loaf pan with margarine.

Remove the dough from the bowl and knead in the sun-dried tomatoes. Knead again for 2–3 minutes.

Place the dough in the pan and let rise for 30–40 minutes or until it has doubled in size again. Bake in a preheated oven, 375°F/190°C, for 30–35 minutes or until golden and the base sounds hollow when tapped. Cool on a wire rack.

COOK'S TIP
You could make mini sun-dried tomato loaves for children. Divide the dough into 8 equal portions, leave to rise, and bake in mini-loaf pans for 20 minutes.

serves 4 | prep 30 mins + 2 hrs rising | cook 40 mins

cheese & potato braid

This bread has a delicious cheese, garlic, and rosemary flavor, and is best eaten straight from the oven. This recipe makes a 1-lb/450-g loaf.

INGREDIENTS
16 oz/75 g mealy potatoes, diced
2 x 1¼ oz/7 g envelopes active
  dry yeast
6 cups white bread flour
1 tbsp salt
2 cups Vegetable Stock (see page 29)
2 garlic cloves, crushed
2 tbsp chopped fresh rosemary
4½ oz/125 g Swiss cheese, grated
1 tbsp vegetable oil

Lightly grease and flour a cookie sheet.

Cook the potatoes in a pan of boiling water for 10 minutes or until soft. Drain and mash the potatoes.

Transfer the mashed potatoes to a large mixing bowl.

Stir the yeast, flour, salt, and stock into the mashed potatoes and mix together to form a smooth dough.

Add the garlic, rosemary, and 2¾ oz/75 g of the cheese and knead the dough for 5 minutes. Make a hollow in the dough, pour in the oil, and knead the dough.

Cover the dough and let rise in a warm place for 1½ hours or until doubled in size.

Knead the dough again and divide it into 3 equal portions. Roll each portion into a 14-inch/35-cm sausage shape.

Pressing one end of each of the sausage shapes together, braid the dough and fold the remaining ends underneath. Place the braid on the cookie sheet, cover, and let rise for 30 minutes.

Sprinkle the remaining cheese over the top of the braid and bake in a preheated oven, at 375°F/190°C, for 40 minutes or until the base of the loaf sounds hollow when tapped. Serve warm.

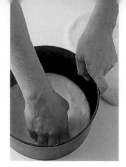

serves 4 | prep 1 hr 45 mins | cook 1 hr 5 mins

roasted bell pepper bread

Bell peppers become wonderfully sweet and mild when they are roasted, and make this bread delicious.

INGREDIENTS
margarine, for greasing
1 red bell pepper, halved and seeded
1 yellow bell pepper, halved and seeded
2 sprigs rosemary
1 tbsp olive oil
¼ oz/7 g dried yeast
1 tsp granulated sugar
1¼ cups lukewarm water
1 lb/450 g white bread flour
1 tsp salt

Grease a 9-inch/23-cm deep circular cake pan with margarine.

Place the bell peppers and rosemary in a shallow roasting pan. Pour over the oil and roast in a preheated oven, 400°F/200°C, for 20 minutes or until slightly charred. Remove the skin from the bell peppers and cut the flesh into slices.

Place the yeast and sugar in a small bowl and mix with ½ cup of lukewarm water. Let the mixture ferment in a warm place for at least 15 minutes.

Sift the flour and salt together into a large bowl. Stir in the yeast mixture and the remaining water and mix to form a smooth dough.

Knead the dough for about 5 minutes until smooth. Cover with oiled plastic wrap and let rise for about 30 minutes or until doubled in size.

Cut the dough into 3 equal portions. Roll the portions into circles slightly larger than the cake pan.

Place 1 circle in the bottom of the pan so that it reaches up the sides of the pan by about ¾ inch/2 cm. Top the dough circle with half of the bell pepper mixture.

Place the second circle of dough on top, followed by the remaining bell pepper mixture. Place the last circle of dough on top, pushing the edges of the dough down the sides of the pan.

Cover the dough with oiled plastic wrap and let rise for 30–40 minutes. Return to the oven and bake for 45 minutes until golden or the bottom sounds hollow when lightly tapped. Transfer to a wire rack to cool slightly, then cut into slices and serve warm.

makes 8 | prep 2 hrs 15 mins | cook 15 mins

sun-dried tomato rolls

These white rolls have the addition of finely chopped sun-dried tomatoes. Use those preserved in jars in olive oil for this recipe.

INGREDIENTS
2 cups white bread flour
½ tsp salt
1 sachet active dry yeast
⅓ cup butter, melted and cooled slightly
3 tbsp milk, warmed
2 eggs, beaten
1¾ oz/50 g sun-dried tomatoes, well
  drained and chopped finely
milk, for brushing

Lightly grease a cookie sheet.

Sift the flour and salt into a large mixing bowl. Stir in the yeast, then pour in the butter, milk, and eggs. Mix together to form a dough.

Turn the dough onto a lightly floured counter and knead for about 5 minutes

Place the dough in a greased bowl, cover, and let rise in a warm place for 1–1½ hours or until the dough has doubled in size. Punch down the dough for approximately 2–3 minutes.

Knead the sun-dried tomatoes into the dough, sprinkling the counter with extra flour as the tomatoes are quite oily.

Divide the dough into 8 balls and place them on the cookie sheet. Cover and leave to rise for about 30 minutes or until the rolls have doubled in size.

Brush the rolls with milk and bake in a preheated oven, 450°F/230°C, for 10–15 minutes or until the rolls are golden brown.

Transfer the rolls to a cooling rack and let cool slightly before serving.

makes 8 | prep 1 hr 45 mins | cook 35 mins

garlic bread rolls

This bread is not at all like the store-bought, ready-made garlic bread. Instead it has a subtle flavor and a soft texture.

INGREDIENTS
butter, for greasing
12 cloves garlic, peeled
1½ cups milk
3½ cups white bread flour
1 tsp salt
1 sachet active dry yeast
1 tbsp dried mixed herbs
2 tbsp sunflower oil
1 egg, beaten lightly
milk, for brushing
rock salt, for sprinkling

Grease a cookie sheet with a little butter and set aside.

Place the garlic cloves and milk in a pan, bring to a boil, and simmer gently for 15 minutes. Let cool slightly, then process in a blender or food processor to blend in the garlic.

Sift the flour and salt into a large mixing bowl, stir in the yeast, then add the mixed herbs to the mixture.

Add the garlic-flavored milk, sunflower oil, and beaten egg to the dry ingredients and mix to form a dough.

Place the dough on a lightly floured counter and knead lightly for a few minutes until smooth and soft.

Place the dough in a greased bowl, cover, and let rise in a warm place for about 1 hour or until doubled in size.

Punch down the dough by kneading it for 2 minutes. Divide the dough into 8 pieces and shape into rolls. Place the rolls on the prepared cookie sheet. Score the top of each roll with a knife, cover, and let stand for 15 minutes.

Brush the rolls with milk and sprinkle rock salt over the top. Bake in a preheated oven, 425°F/220°C, for 15–20 minutes.

Transfer the rolls to a cooling rack and let cool before serving.

makes 2 | prep 10 mins | cook 20 mins

pizza margherita

With its red, white, and green ingredients—the colors of the Italian flag—this pizza was created to honor Queen Margherita. While it is delicious with just this simple topping, it can also be used as a basis for more elaborate pizzas with extra ingredients.

INGREDIENTS
**1 quantity Basic Pizza Dough
   (see page 24)**

for the topping
6 tomatoes, sliced thinly
**6 oz/175 g mozzarella cheese, drained and
   sliced thinly**
salt and pepper
2 tbsp shredded fresh basil leaves
2 tbsp olive oil

Turn out the Basic Pizza Dough onto a lightly floured counter and punch down. Knead briefly, then cut it in half and roll out each piece into a circle about ¼ inch/5 mm thick.

Transfer to a lightly oiled cookie sheet and push up the edges with your fingers to form a small rim.

For the topping, arrange the tomato and mozzarella slices alternately over the pizza bases. Season to taste with salt and pepper, sprinkle with the basil, and drizzle with the olive oil.

Bake in a preheated oven, 450°F/230°C, for 15–20 minutes, until the crust is crisp and the cheese has melted. Serve immediately.

VARIATION
For Pizza Napoletana, first spread each pizza base with 4½ teaspoons tomato paste, then top with the tomato and cheese slices. Arrange halved, drained, canned anchovy fillets in a pattern on top, season to taste with pepper, drizzle with olive oil, and bake as above.

makes 1 | prep 1 hr 15 mins | cook 30 mins

tomato & ricotta pizza

This is a traditional dish from the Calabrian Mountains in southern Italy, where it is made with naturally sun-dried tomatoes and ricotta cheese.

INGREDIENTS
1 quantity Basic Pizza Dough (see page 24)

for the topping
4 tbsp sun-dried tomato paste
⅔ cup ricotta cheese
10 sun-dried tomatoes in oil, drained
1 tbsp fresh thyme
salt and pepper

Knead the Basic Pizza Dough on a lightly floured counter for 2 minutes.

Using a rolling pin, roll out the dough to form a circle, then carefully transfer it to an oiled cookie sheet, pushing out the edges until even. The dough should be no more than about ¼ inch/5 mm thick because it will rise during cooking.

Spread the sun-dried tomato paste evenly over the dough, then add spoonfuls of ricotta cheese, dotting them over the pizza.

Cut the sun-dried tomatoes into strips and arrange these on top of the pizza.

Sprinkle the thyme over the top of the pizza and season with salt and pepper to taste. Bake in a preheated oven, 400°F/200°C, for 30 minutes or until piping hot with a golden crust. Serve the pizza at once.

makes 1 | prep 1 hr 15 mins | cook 40 mins

onion, prosciutto & cheese pizza

This pizza was a favorite of the Romans. It is slightly unusual because the topping is made without a tomato sauce base.

INGREDIENTS
1 quantity Basic Pizza Dough (see page 24)

for the topping
2 tbsp olive oil
9 oz/250 g onions, sliced into rings
2 garlic cloves, crushed
1 red bell pepper, diced
3½ oz/100 g prosciutto, cut into strips
3½ oz/100 g mozzarella cheese, sliced
2 tbsp rosemary, stalks removed and roughly chopped

Knead the Basic Pizza Dough on a lightly floured counter for 2 minutes.

Using a rolling pin, roll out the dough to form a square shape, then place it on an oiled cookie sheet, pushing out the edges until even. The dough should be no more than ¼ inch/5 mm thick because it will rise during cooking.

To make the topping, heat the oil in a skillet. Add the onions and garlic and cook for 3 minutes. Add the bell pepper and fry for 2 minutes.

Cover the skillet and cook the vegetables over a low heat for 10 minutes, stirring occasionally, until the onions are slightly caramelized. Leave to cool slightly.

Spread the topping evenly over the pizza base. Arrange the prosciutto, mozzarella, and rosemary over the top.

Bake in a preheated oven, 400°F/200°C, for 20–25 minutes. Serve hot.

VARIATION
To ring the changes with this pizza, use cooked ham (prosciutto cotto) instead of the prosciutto and add 2½ oz/70 g white mushrooms to the onion and garlic mixture before adding the bell pepper. Use red onions instead of white to add extra color to the pizza.

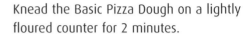

makes 1 | prep 1 hr 15 mins | cook 45 mins

mushroom pizza

Juicy mushrooms and stringy mozzarella top this tomato-based pizza. Use wild mushrooms or a combination of wild and cultivated mushrooms.

INGREDIENTS
1 quantity Basic Pizza Dough (see page 24)

for the topping
14 oz/400g canned chopped tomatoes
2 garlic cloves, crushed
1 tsp dried basil
1 tbsp olive oil
2 tbsp tomato paste
7 oz/200 g mushrooms
5½ oz/150 g mozzarella cheese, grated
salt and pepper
basil leaves, to garnish

Knead the Basic Pizza Dough on a lightly floured counter for 2 minutes.

Using a rolling pin, roll out the dough to form an oval or a circular shape, then place it on an oiled cookie sheet, pushing out the edges until even. The dough should be no more than ¼ inch/5 mm thick because it will rise during cooking.

Using a sharp knife, chop the mushrooms into slices.

To make the topping, place the tomatoes, garlic, dried basil, olive oil, and salt and pepper in a large pan and simmer for 20 minutes or until the sauce has thickened.

Stir in the tomato paste and let the sauce cool slightly.

Spread the sauce over the base of the pizza, top with the mushrooms, and scatter over the mozzarella.

Bake in a preheated oven, 400°F/200°C, for 25 minutes. Garnish with basil leaves and serve.

makes 1 | prep 1 hr 45 mins | cook 20 mins

cheese & artichoke pizza

Sliced artichoke hearts combined with sharp Cheddar, tangy Parmesan, and bleu cheese give a really delicious topping to this pizza.

INGREDIENTS
1 quantity Basic Pizza Dough (see page 24)

for the topping
Basic Tomato Sauce (see page 26)
2 oz/60 g bleu cheese, sliced
4½ oz/125 g artichoke hearts in oil, sliced
½ small red onion, chopped
1½ oz/45 g sharp Cheddar cheese, grated
2 tbsp freshly grated Parmesan
1 tbsp chopped fresh thyme
oil from artichokes for drizzling
salt and pepper

to serve
salad leaves
cherry tomatoes, halved

Roll out or press the dough, using a rolling pin or your hands, to form a 25-cm/10-inch circle on a lightly floured counter.

Place the pizza base on a large greased cookie sheet or pizza pan and push up the edge slightly. Cover and leave to rise for 10 minutes in a warm place.

Spread the tomato sauce almost to the edge of the base. Arrange the bleu cheese on top of the sauce, followed by the artichoke hearts and red onion.

Mix the Cheddar and Parmesan cheeses together with the thyme and sprinkle the

mixture over the pizza. Drizzle a little of the oil from the jar of artichokes over the pizza and season to taste.

Bake in a preheated oven, 400°F/200°C, for 18–20 minutes, or until the edge is crisp and golden and the cheese is bubbling.

Mix the fresh salad leaves and cherry tomato halves together and serve with the pizza, cut into slices.

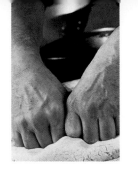

makes 1 | prep 1 hr 45 mins | cook 1 hr

four seasons pizza

This pizza is divided into 4 sections, each with a different topping, to represent the 4 seasons. You can vary the toppings according to taste.

INGREDIENTS
1 quantity Basic Pizza Dough (see page 24)
all-purpose flour, for dusting

for the tomato sauce
2 tbsp olive oil
1 small onion, chopped finely
1 garlic clove, chopped finely
1 red bell pepper, seeded and chopped
8 oz/225 g plum tomatoes, peeled
  (see Cook's Tip, page 111) and chopped
1 tbsp tomato paste
1 tsp soft brown sugar
1 tbsp shredded fresh basil leaves
1 bay leaf
salt and pepper

for the topping
2½ oz/70 g drained bottled clams or drained
  anchovy fillets, halved lengthwise, or
  cooked shelled shrimp
2 oz/55 g baby globe artichokes or artichoke
  hearts, sliced thinly, or canned asparagus
  spears, drained
1 oz/25 g mozzarella cheese, drained and
  sliced thinly
1 tomato, sliced thinly
3½ oz/100 g mushrooms or pepperoni,
  sliced thinly
2 tsp capers, rinsed
2 tsp pitted, sliced black olives
2 tbsp olive oil, plus extra for brushing
salt and pepper

To make the tomato sauce, heat the olive oil in a heavy-bottom pan. Add the onion, garlic, and bell pepper, and cook over low heat, stirring occasionally, for 5 minutes, until softened. Add the tomatoes, tomato paste, sugar, basil, and bay leaf, and season to taste with salt and pepper. Cover and let simmer, stirring occasionally, for 30 minutes, until thickened. Remove the pan from the heat and let the sauce cool completely.

Turn out the prepared pizza dough onto a lightly floured counter and punch down. Knead briefly, then cut it in half and roll out each piece into a circle about ¼ inch/5 mm thick. Transfer to a lightly oiled cookie sheet and push up the edges with your fingers to form a small rim.

Spread the tomato sauce over the pizza bases, almost to the edge. Cover one-quarter with clams, anchovy fillets, or shrimp. Cover a second quarter with sliced artichokes, artichoke hearts, or asparagus spears. Cover the third quarter with alternate slices of mozzarella and tomato. Cover the final quarter with sliced mushrooms or pepperoni. Sprinkle the surface with capers and olives, season to taste with salt and pepper, and drizzle with olive oil.

Bake in a preheated oven, 425°F/220°C, for 20–25 minutes, until the crust is crisp and the cheese has melted. Serve immediately.

VARIATION
Other toppings, either used in combination or singly, could include: mixed seafood, such as shrimp, mussels, and squid rings; roasted Mediterranean vegetables, say eggplants, bell peppers, tomatoes, zucchinis, and red onions; exotic mushrooms and pine nuts; or hot pepperoni and chilies.

makes 1 | prep 20 mins | cook 55 mins

pissaladière

This is a variation of the classic Italian pizza but is made with ready-made pie dough. It is perfect for outdoor eating.

INGREDIENTS
4 tbsp olive oil
1 lb 9 oz/700 g red onions, sliced thinly
2 garlic cloves, crushed
2 tsp superfine sugar
2 tbsp red wine vinegar
12 oz/350 g fresh ready-made pie dough
salt and pepper

for the topping
2 x 1¾ oz/50 g cans anchovy fillets
12 green olives, pitted
1 tsp dried marjoram

Lightly grease a jelly roll pan. Heat the olive oil in a large pan. Add the red onions and garlic and cook over a low heat for about 30 minutes, stirring occasionally.

Add the sugar and red wine vinegar to the pan and season with plenty of salt and pepper.

On a lightly floured counter, roll out the pie dough to a rectangle, about 13 x 9 inches/33 x 23 cm. Place the pie dough rectangle onto the prepared pan, pushing the pie dough into the corners of the pan.

Spread the onion mixture over the pie dough. Arrange the anchovy fillets and green olives on top, then sprinkle the pie with the marjoram.

Bake in a preheated oven, 425°F/220°C, for 20-25 minutes or until the pissaladière is lightly golden. Serve the pissaladière piping hot, straight from the oven.

COOK'S TIP
Cut the pissaladière into squares or triangles for easy finger food at a party or grill.

makes 4 | prep 1 hr 30 mins | cook 40 mins

vegetable calzone

These pizza base parcels are great for making in advance and freezing—they can be defrosted when required for a quick snack.

INGREDIENTS
for the dough
3½ cups white bread flour
2 tsp active dry yeast
1 tsp superfine sugar
¾ cup Vegetable Stock (see page 29)
¾ cup sieved tomatoes
beaten egg

for the filling
1 tbsp vegetable oil
1 onion, chopped
1 garlic clove, crushed
2 tbsp chopped sun-dried tomatoes
3½ oz/100 g spinach, chopped
3 tbsp canned and drained corn
¼ cup green beans, cut into 3
1 tbsp tomato paste
1 tbsp chopped oregano
1¾ oz/50 g mozzarella cheese, sliced
salt and pepper

Sift the flour into a bowl. Add the yeast and sugar and beat in the stock and sieved tomatoes to make a smooth dough.

Knead the dough on a lightly floured counter for 10 minutes, then place in a clean, lightly oiled bowl and let rise in a warm place for 1 hour.

Heat the oil in a skillet and sauté the onion for 2–3 minutes.

Stir in the garlic, tomatoes, spinach, corn, and beans and cook for 3–4 minutes. Add the tomato paste and oregano and season with salt and pepper to taste.

Divide the risen dough into 4 equal portions and roll each onto a floured counter to form an 7-inch/18-cm circle.

Spoon a quarter of the filling on to one half of each circle and top with cheese. Fold the dough over to encase the filling, sealing the edge with a fork. Glaze with beaten egg. Put the calzone on a lightly greased cookie sheet and cook in a preheated oven, 425°F/220°C, for 25–30 minutes until risen and golden. Serve warm.

makes 4 | prep 1 hr 30 mins | cook 35 mins

potato & tomato calzone

These pizza dough Italian pasties are best served hot with a salad as a delicious lunch or supper dish.

INGREDIENTS
for the dough
4 cups white bread flour
1 tsp active dry yeast
1¼ cups Vegetable Stock (see page 29)
1 tbsp clear honey
1 tsp caraway seeds
milk, for glazing

for the filling
8 oz/225 g waxy potatoes, diced
1 tbsp vegetable oil
1 onion, halved and sliced
2 garlic cloves, crushed
1½ oz/40 g sun-dried tomatoes
2 tbsp chopped fresh basil
2 tbsp tomato paste
2 celery sticks, sliced
1¾ oz/50 g mozzarella cheese, grated

To make the dough, sift the flour into a large bowl and stir in the yeast. Make a well in the center of the mixture.

Stir in the vegetable stock, honey, and caraway seeds and bring the mixture together to form a dough.

Turn the dough out onto a lightly floured counter and knead for 8 minutes until smooth. Place the dough in a lightly oiled mixing bowl, cover, and let rise in a warm place for 1 hour or until it has doubled in size.

Meanwhile, make the filling. Heat the oil in a skillet and add all of the remaining ingredients except for the cheese. Cook for 5 minutes, stirring constantly.

Divide the risen dough into 4 pieces. On a lightly floured counter, roll them out to form four 7-inch/18-cm circles. Spoon equal amounts of the filling onto one half of each circle.

Sprinkle the cheese over the filling. Brush the edges of the dough with milk and fold the dough over to form 4 semi-circles, pressing to seal the edges.

Place on a non-stick cookie sheet and brush with milk. Cook in a preheated oven, 425°F/220°C, for 30 minutes until golden and risen. Serve hot.

makes 1 | prep 1 hr 30 mins | cook 25 mins

seafood pizza

*Bags of fresh mixed seafood, containing shrimp, squid rings, mussels, and other shellfish are available from the chiller cabinets of many supermarkets.
They tend to have a better flavor and texture than frozen seafood.*

INGREDIENTS
1 quantity Basic Pizza Dough (see page 24)
virgin olive oil, for greasing and drizzling

for the topping
1 quantity Basic Tomato Sauce (see page 26)
8 oz/225 g mixed fresh* seafood
½ red bell pepper, seeded and chopped
½ yellow bell pepper, seeded and chopped
1 tbsp capers, rinsed
2 oz/55 g Taleggio cheese, grated
3 tbsp freshly grated Parmesan cheese
½ tsp dried oregano
2¾ oz/75 g anchovy fillets in oil,
    drained and sliced
10 black olives, pitted
salt and pepper

Turn out the Basic Pizza Dough onto a lightly floured counter and punch down. Knead briefly, then roll out the dough into a circle about ¼ inch/5 mm thick. Transfer to a lightly oiled cookie sheet and push up the edge with your fingers to form a small rim.

Spread the tomato sauce over the pizza base, almost to the edge. Arrange the mixed seafood, red and yellow bell peppers, and capers evenly on top.

Sprinkle the Taleggio, Parmesan, and oregano evenly over the topping. Add the anchovy fillets and olives, drizzle with olive oil, and season to taste with salt and pepper.

Bake in a preheated oven, 425°F/220°C, for 20–25 minutes, until the crust is crisp and the cheese has melted. Serve immediately.

COOK'S TIP
If you have to use frozen mixed seafood, make sure that it is completely thawed first.

makes 8 | prep 1 hr 15 mins | cook 15 mins

mini pizzas

Pizzette, as they are known in Italy, are tiny pizzas. This quantity will make 8 individual pizzas, or 16 cocktail pizzas to go with drinks.

INGREDIENTS
1 quantity Basic Pizza Dough (see page 24)

for the topping
2 zucchinis
3½ oz/100 g sieved tomatoes
2¾ oz/75 g pancetta,* diced
1¾ oz/50 g black olives,*
   pitted and chopped
1 tbsp mixed dried herbs
2 tbsp olive oil

Turn the Basic Pizza Dough out onto a floured counter.

Knead the dough for 2 minutes and divide it into 8 balls.

Roll out each portion thinly to form circles or squares, then place them on an oiled cookie sheet, pushing out the edges until even. The dough should be no more than ¼ inch/5 mm thick because it will rise during cooking.

To make the topping, grate the zucchinis finely. Cover with paper towels and leave to stand for 10 minutes to absorb some of the zucchini juices.

Spread 2–3 teaspoons of the sieved tomatoes over the pizza bases and top each with the grated zucchinis, pancetta, and olives.

Season with pepper to taste, a sprinkling of mixed dried herbs and drizzle with olive oil.

Bake in a preheated oven, 400°F/200°C, for 15 minutes or until crispy. Season with salt and pepper to taste and serve hot.

VARIATIONS
*You can use smoked pancetta if you want your pizzette to have a more intense flavor. Green olives can be substituted for the stronger-tasting black olives, although the pizzas will have less color contrast.

part five

DOLCI
desserts, cakes & cookies

Creamy or fruity desserts, tarts, cakes, ice creams

and sherbets, and cookies are the grand finale in

the Italian menu. They are served on special

occasions but you should always be able to find

an excuse for making one of the delicious sweet

creations found here!

serves 4 | prep 5 mins | cook 15 mins

zabaglione

This well-known dish is really a light but rich egg mousse flavored with Marsala.

INGREDIENTS
5 egg yolks
3½ oz/100 g superfine sugar
⅔ cup Marsala or
    sweet sherry
amaretti cookies, to serve
    (optional)

Place the egg yolks in a large mixing bowl.

Add the superfine sugar to the egg yolks and whisk until the mixture is thick and very pale and has doubled in volume.

Place the bowl containing the egg yolk and sugar mixture over a pan of gently simmering water.

Add the Marsala or sherry to the egg yolk and sugar mixture and continue whisking until the foam mixture becomes warm. This process may take as long as 10 minutes.

Pour the mixture, which should be frothy and light, into 4 wine glasses.

Serve the zabaglione warm with fresh fruit or amaretti cookies, if you wish.

serves 6 | prep 25 mins + 8 hrs chilling | cook 10 mins

coffee panna cotta with chocolate sauce

Panna cotta literally means «cooked cream.» Flavoring it with coffee and serving it with a chocolate sauce adds a new look to this popular Italian dessert.

INGREDIENTS
oil, for brushing
2½ cups heavy cream
1 vanilla bean
generous ¼ cup golden superfine sugar
2 tsp instant espresso coffee granules, dissolved in 4 tbsp water
2 tsp powdered gelatin
chocolate-covered coffee beans, to serve

for the sauce
⅔ cup light cream
2 oz/55 g semisweet chocolate, melted

Lightly brush 6 x ⅔-cup/150-ml molds with oil. Place the cream in a pan. Split the vanilla bean and scrape the black seeds into the cream. Add the vanilla bean and the sugar, then heat gently until almost boiling. Strain the cream into a heatproof bowl and set aside. Place the coffee in a small heat-proof bowl, sprinkle on the gelatin and let stand for 5 minutes, or until spongy. Set the bowl over a pan of gently simmering water until the gelatin has dissolved.

Stir a little of the reserved cream into the gelatin mixture, then stir the gelatin mixture into the remainder of the cream.

Divide the mixture between the prepared molds and let cool, then let chill in the refrigerator for 8 hours, or overnight.

To make the sauce, place a quarter of the cream in a bowl and stir in the melted chocolate. Gradually stir in the remaining cream, reserving 1 tablespoon. To serve the panna cotta, dip the base of the molds briefly into hot water and turn out onto 6 dessert plates. Pour the chocolate cream round. Dot drops of the reserved cream onto the sauce and feather it with a toothpick. Decorate with chocolate-covered coffee beans and serve.

serves 8 | prep 30 mins + 3 hrs chilling | cook 30 mins

tiramisù

Tiramisù is an Italian version of the British trifle. A wicked combination of mascarpone, chocolate, coffee, and rum makes this delicious dessert very rich and quite irresistible!

INGREDIENTS
butter, for greasing
3 eggs
¾ cup golden superfine sugar
⅔ cup self-rising flour
1 tbsp unsweetened cocoa
⅔ cup cold black coffee
2 tbsp rum
2 tsp unsweetened cocoa, to decorate

for the filling
1⅝ cups mascarpone cheese
1 cup fresh custard
¼ cup golden superfine sugar
3½ oz/100 g semisweet
  chocolate, grated

Preheat the oven to 350°F/180°C. To make the cake, grease an 8-inch/20-cm round cake pan with butter and line with parchment paper. Place the eggs and sugar in a large bowl and beat together until thick and light. Sift the flour and unsweetened cocoa over the batter and fold in gently. Spoon the batter into the prepared pan and bake in the oven for 30 minutes, or until the cake springs back when pressed gently in the center. Let stand in the pan for 5 minutes, then turn out onto a cooling rack.

Place the black coffee and rum in a bowl or cup, mix together, and set aside. To make the filling, place the mascarpone in a large bowl and beat until soft. Stir in the custard, then gradually add the sugar, beating constantly. Stir in the grated chocolate.

Cut the cake horizontally into 3 layers and place 1 layer on a serving plate. Sprinkle with one-third of the coffee mixture, then cover with one-third of the mascarpone mixture. Repeat the layers, finishing with a topping of the mascarpone mixture. Let chill in the refrigerator for 3 hours. Sift over the unsweetened cocoa before serving.

VARIATION
To save time, use ladyfingers instead of cake. Dip the ladyfingers in coffee and layer them with the mascarpone mixture in a bowl.

pear tart

serves 6 | prep 1 hr + 1 hr chilling | cook 50 mins

Pears are a very popular fruit in Italy. In this recipe from Trentino they are flavored with almonds, cinnamon, raisins, and apricot preserve.

INGREDIENTS
2¼ cups all-purpose flour
pinch of salt
½ cup superfine sugar
½ cup butter, diced
1 egg
1 egg yolk
few drops of vanilla extract
2–3 tsp water
sifted confectioners' sugar, for sprinkling

for the filling
4 tbsp apricot preserve
2 oz/60 g amaretti or ratafia cookies, crumbled
1¾–2 lb 4 oz/850 g–1 kg pears, peeled and cored
1 tsp ground cinnamon
½ cup raisins
⅓ cup soft brown sugar

Sift the flour and salt onto a flat surface, make a well in the center, and add the sugar, butter, egg, egg yolk, vanilla extract, and most of the water.

Using your fingers, gradually work the flour into the other ingredients to give a smooth dough, adding more water if necessary. Wrap in plastic wrap and chill until firm (about 1 hour). Alternatively, put all the ingredients into a food processor and work until smooth.

Roll out three-quarters of the dough and use to line a shallow 10-inch/25-cm cake pan or deep tart pan. Spread the apricot preserve over the base and sprinkle with the crushed cookies.

Slice the pears very thinly. Arrange over the cookies in the pie case. Sprinkle with cinnamon, then with raisins, and finally with brown sugar.

Roll out a thin sausage shape using one-third of the remaining dough, and place around the edge of the pie. Roll the remainder into thin sausages and arrange in a lattice over the pie, 4 or 5 strips in each direction, attaching them to the strip around the edge.

Cook in a preheated oven, 400°F/200°C, for 50 minutes or until golden and cooked through. Let cool, then serve warm or chilled, lightly sprinkled with sifted confectioners' sugar.

serves 6-8 | prep 1 hr + 30 mins chilling | cook 55 mins

ricotta cheesecake

This melt-in-the-mouth cheesecake confirms the belief that all the best Italian desserts come from Sicily.

INGREDIENTS
for the pastry
**1⅛ cups all-purpose flour, plus extra
    for dusting**
3 tbsp superfine sugar
salt
**4 oz/115 g unsalted butter,
    chilled and diced**
1 egg yolk

for the filling
1 lb/450 g ricotta cheese
½ cup heavy cream
2 eggs, plus 1 egg yolk
⅜ cup superfine sugar
finely grated rind of 1 lemon
finely grated rind of 1 orange

To make the pastry, sift the flour with the sugar and a pinch of salt onto a counter and make a well in the center. Add the diced butter and egg yolk to the well and, using your fingertips, gradually work in the flour mixture until fully incorporated.

Gather up the dough and knead very lightly. Cut off about one quarter of the kneaded dough, wrap in plastic wrap, and let chill in the refrigerator. Press the remaining dough into the base of the tart pan and let chill for 30 minutes.

To make the filling, beat the ricotta with the cream, eggs and extra egg yolk, sugar, lemon

rind, and orange rind. Cover with plastic wrap and set aside in the refrigerator until needed.

Prick the base of the pastry shell all over with a fork. Line with foil, fill with pie weights, and bake blind in a preheated oven, 375°F/190°C, for 15 minutes.

Remove the pastry shell from the oven and take out the foil and pie weights. Stand the pan on a cooling rack and set aside.

Spoon the ricotta mixture into the pastry shell and level the surface. Roll out the reserved pastry on a lightly floured counter and cut it into strips. Arrange the strips over the filling in a lattice pattern, brushing the overlapping ends with water so that they stick.

Bake in the preheated oven for 30–35 minutes, until the top of the cheesecake is golden and the filling has set. Let cool on a cooling rack before lifting off the side of the pan. Cut into wedges to serve.

serves 6 | prep 15 mins + 3–48 hrs chilling | cook 20 mins

caramelized oranges

The secret of these oranges is to allow them to marinate in the syrup for at least 24 hours, so the flavors amalgamate.

INGREDIENTS
6 large oranges
1 cup sugar
1 cup water
6 whole cloves (optional)
2–4 tbsp orange-flavored liqueur
  or brandy

Using a citrus zester or potato peeler, pare the rind from 2 of the oranges in narrow strips without any white pith attached. If using a potato peeler, cut the peel into very thin julienne strips.

Put the orange strips into a small pan and barely cover with water. Bring to a boil and simmer for 5 minutes. Drain the strips and reserve the water.

Cut away all the white pith and peel from the remaining oranges using a very sharp knife, then cut horizontally into 4 slices. Reassemble the oranges and hold in place with toothpicks. Stand in a heatproof dish.

Put the sugar and water into a heavy-bottom pan with the cloves, if using. Bring to a boil and simmer gently until the sugar has dissolved, then boil hard without stirring until the syrup thickens and begins to color. Continue to cook until a light golden brown, then quickly remove from the heat and carefully pour in the reserved orange rind liquid.

Place over gentle heat until the caramel has fully dissolved again, then remove from the heat and add the liqueur or brandy. Pour the syrup over the oranges.

Sprinkle the orange strips over the oranges, cover with plastic wrap and let stand until cold. Chill for at least 3 hours and preferably for 24–48 hours before serving. If time allows, spoon the syrup over the oranges several times while they are marinating. Discard the toothpicks before serving.

serves 4 | prep 20 mins + 1 hr 20 mins chilling | cook 0 mins

sweet mascarpone mousse

This sweet cream cheese dessert is a perfect complement to the tartness of fresh summer fruits.

INGREDIENTS
1 lb/450 g mascarpone cheese
3½ oz/100 g superfine sugar
4 egg yolks
14 oz/400 g frozen summer fruits, such as raspberries and red currants
red currants, to garnish
amaretti cookies, to serve

Place the mascarpone in a large mixing bowl. Using a wooden spoon, beat the mascarpone until quite smooth.

Stir the egg yolks and sugar into the mascarpone, mixing well. Let the mixture chill in the refrigerator for 1 hour.

Spoon a layer of the mascarpone mixture into the bottom of 4 individual serving dishes. Spoon a layer of the summer fruits on top of the mixture. Repeat the layers in the same order, reserving some of the mascarpone mixture for the top.

Leave the mousses to chill in the refrigerator for about 20 minutes. The fruits should still be slightly frozen.

Garnish the mascarpone mousses with red currants and serve with amaretti cookies.

serves 4 | prep 15 mins + 30 mins chilling | cook 25 mins

italian bread pudding

This deliciously rich pudding is cooked with cream and apples and is delicately flavored with orange.

INGREDIENTS
1 tbsp butter
2 small eating apples, peeled, cored, and
  sliced into rings
2¾ oz/75 g granulated sugar
2 tbsp white wine
3½ oz/100 g white bread, sliced, with
  crusts removed (slightly stale French
  baguette is ideal)
1¼ cups light cream
2 eggs, beaten
pared rind of 1 orange, cut into short sticks

Lightly grease a 2-pint/1.2-liter deep heat-proof dish with the butter.

Arrange the apple rings in the base of the dish. Sprinkle half of the sugar evenly over the apples.

Pour the wine over the apples. Add the bread slices, pushing them down with your hands to flatten them slightly.

Mix the cream with the eggs, the remaining sugar, and the orange rind and pour the mixture over the bread. Leave to soak for 30 minutes.

Bake the pudding in a preheated oven, 350°F/180°C, for 25 minutes until golden and set. Serve warm.

makes 16 | prep 30 mins + 1 hr rising | cook 20 mins

baked sweet ravioli

These scrumptious little parcels are the perfect dessert for anyone with a really sweet tooth.

INGREDIENTS
for the sweet pasta dough
3¾ cups all purpose flour
**10 tbsp butter, plus extra
   for greasing**
¾ cup superfine sugar
4 eggs
1 oz/25 g yeast
4 fl oz/125 ml warm milk

for the filling
⅔ cup chestnut paste
½ cup unsweetened cocoa
¼ cup superfine sugar
½ cup chopped almonds
1 cup crushed amaretti cookies
⅝ cup orange marmalade

To make the sweet pasta dough, sift the flour into a mixing bowl, then mix in the butter, sugar, and 3 eggs.

Mix together the yeast and warm milk in a small bowl and, when thoroughly combined, mix into the dough.

Knead the dough for 20 minutes, cover with a clean cloth and set aside in a warm place for 1 hour to rise.

Mix together the chestnut paste, unsweetened cocoa, sugar, almonds, crushed amaretti cookies, and orange marmalade in a separate bowl.

Grease a cookie sheet with butter.

Lightly flour a counter. Roll out the pasta dough into a thin sheet and cut into 2-inch/5-cm rounds with a plain pastry cutter.

Put a spoonful of filling onto each round and then fold in half, pressing the edges to seal. Arrange on the prepared cookie sheet, spacing the ravioli out well.

Beat the remaining egg and brush all over the ravioli to glaze. Bake in a preheated oven, 350°F/180°C, for 20 minutes. Serve hot.

serves 4 | prep 20 mins + 1–2 hrs chilling | cook 0 mins

mascarpone creams

Rich and self-indulgent, these creamy desserts make the perfect end to a special-occasion meal.

INGREDIENTS
4 oz/115 g amaretti cookies, crushed*
4 tbsp amaretto or maraschino
4 eggs, separated
generous ¼ cup superfine sugar
1 cup mascarpone cheese
toasted slivered almonds, to decorate

Place the amaretti crumbs in a bowl, add the amaretto or Maraschino and set aside to soak.

Meanwhile, beat the egg yolks with the superfine sugar until pale and thick. Fold in the mascarpone and soaked cookie crumbs.

Whisk the egg white in a separate, spotlessly clean, bowl until stiff, then gently fold into the cheese mixture. Divide the mascarpone cream between 4 serving dishes and let chill for 1–2 hours. Sprinkle with toasted slivered almonds just before serving.

COOK'S TIP
*The easiest way to make cookie crumbs is to place the cookies in a plastic bag and crush them with a rolling pin.

serves 6 | prep 20 mins | cook 30 mins

stuffed peaches

Peaches grow throughout central and southern Italy—in fact this recipe comes from Piedmont in the northwest.

INGREDIENTS
2 oz/55 g unsalted butter, plus extra for greasing
6 large peaches*
¼ cup ground almonds
2 oz/55 g amaretti cookies, crushed coarsely
1 tbsp amaretto
½ tsp grated lemon rind
1 tsp unsweetened cocoa
2 tsp confectioners' sugar
1 cup medium-dry white wine

Grease a heatproof dish with butter. Cut the peaches in half and remove and discard the pits. Widen the central cavity by cutting away and reserving some of the flesh in a bowl.

Add the almonds, amaretti, amaretto, lemon rind, and half the butter to the reserved peach flesh and mash with a fork. Fill the peach cavities with this mixture and place them in the dish.

Dot the peaches with the remaining butter and sprinkle with the unsweetened cocoa and confectioners' sugar. Pour the wine into the dish and bake in a preheated oven, 350°F/180°C, for 30 minutes, until golden. Serve immediately.

serves 4 | prep 35 mins | cook 2 mins

panettone & strawberries

Panettone is a sweet Italian bread. It is delicious toasted, and when it is topped with mascarpone and strawberries it makes a sumptuous dessert.

INGREDIENTS
8 oz/225 g strawberries
1 oz/25 g superfine sugar
6 tbsp Marsala
½ tsp ground cinnamon
4 slices panettone
4 tbsp mascarpone cheese

Hull and slice the strawberries and place them in a bowl. Add the sugar, Marsala, and cinnamon to the strawberries.

Toss the strawberries in the sugar and cinnamon mixture until they are well coated. Leave to chill in the refrigerator for at least 30 minutes.

When ready to serve, transfer the slices of panettone to a rack set over medium hot coals. Grill the panettone for about 1 minute on each side or until golden brown.

Carefully remove the panettone from the grill and transfer to serving plates.

Top each slice of the panettone with mascarpone and the marinated strawberries. Serve immediately.

serves 6 | prep 30 mins + 6–8 hrs chilling/cooling | cook 20 mins

zucotto

Zucotto is a traditional Italian dessert that combines those natural partners, semisweet chocolate and black cherries.

INGREDIENTS
4 oz/115 g soft margarine, plus
  extra for greasing
scant ⅔ cup self-rising flour
2 tbsp unsweetened cocoa
½ tsp baking powder
generous ½ cup golden superfine sugar
2 eggs, beaten
3 tbsp brandy
2 tbsp Kirsch

for the filling
1¼ cups heavy cream
¼ cup confectioners' sugar, sifted
¼ cup toasted almonds, chopped
8 oz/225 g black cherries, pitted
2 oz/55 g semisweet chocolate,
  chopped finely

to decorate
1 tbsp unsweetened cocoa
1 tbsp confectioners' sugar
fresh cherries

VARIATION
If fresh cherries are not available, use drained canned cherries instead. Replace the Kirsch with an almond-flavored liqueur, such as amaretto.

Preheat the oven to 375°F/190°C. Grease a 12 x 9-inch/30 x 23-cm jelly roll pan with margarine and line with parchment paper. Sift the flour, cocoa, and baking powder into a bowl. Add the sugar, margarine, and eggs. Beat together until well mixed, then spoon into the prepared pan. Bake in the preheated oven for 15–20 minutes, or until well risen and firm to the touch. Let stand in the pan for 5 minutes, then turn out onto a cooling rack.

Using the rim of a 5-cup/1.2-liter heatproof bowl as a guide, cut a circle from the cake and set aside. Line the bowl with plastic wrap. Use the remaining cake, cutting it as necessary, to line the bowl. Place the brandy and Kirsch in a small bowl and mix together. Sprinkle over the cake, including the reserved circle.

To make the filling, pour the cream into a separate bowl and add the confectioners' sugar. Whip until thick, then fold in the almonds, cherries, and chocolate. Fill the sponge mold with the cream mixture and press the cake circle on top. Cover with a plate and a weight, and let chill in the refrigerator for 6–8 hours, or overnight. When ready to serve, turn the zucotto out onto a serving plate. Decorate with cocoa and confectioners' sugar, sifted over in alternating segments, and a few cherries.

makes 8 slices | prep 25 mins + 8 hrs chilling | cook 40 mins

sicilian cassata

This rich cake, with a filling of ricotta cheese, candied fruit, chopped nuts, and chocolate, is a Sicilian specialty.

INGREDIENTS
6 oz/175 g butter, softened,
   plus extra for greasing
scant 1 cup self-rising flour
2 tbsp unsweetened cocoa
1 tsp baking powder
generous 1 cup golden
   superfine sugar
3 eggs
confectioners' sugar, for dusting
chocolate curls,* to decorate

for the filling
1 lb/450 g ricotta cheese
3½ oz/100 g bittersweet chocolate, grated
generous ½ cup golden superfine sugar
3 tbsp Marsala
⅓ cup chopped candied peel
1 oz/25 g almonds, chopped

Preheat the oven to 375°F/190°C. Grease and line the base of a 7-inch/18-cm round cake pan. Sift the flour, cocoa, and baking powder into a large bowl. Add the butter, sugar, and eggs and beat together until smooth and creamy. Pour the mixture into the pan and bake in the preheated oven for 30–40 minutes, until well risen and firm to the touch. Turn out onto a cooling rack after 5 minutes to cool completely.

Wash and dry the cake pan and grease and line it again. To make the filling, rub the ricotta through a strainer into a bowl. Add the grated chocolate, sugar, and Marsala and beat together thoroughly until the mixture is light and fluffy. Stir in the candied peel and almonds.

Cut the thin crust off the top of the cake and discard. Cut the cake horizontally into 3 layers. Place the first slice in the prepared pan and cover with half the ricotta mixture. Repeat the layers, finishing with a cake layer. Press down lightly, cover with a plate and a weight, and leave to chill in the refrigerator for 8 hours, or overnight. To serve, turn the cake out onto a serving plate. Dust with confectioners' sugar and decorate with chocolate curls.

COOK'S TIP
*To make chocolate curls, spread a thin layer of melted chocolate onto a flat surface. Just when it appears to have set, but is still soft, hold a knife or scraper at a 45-degree angle to the surface and push it along to form long scrolls. As the curls form, lift them carefully with the point of a knife

makes 12–14 slices | prep 25 mins | cook 1 hr

almond cake

This rich cake is delicious served with fruit as a dessert or simply with a cup of coffee for a mid-morning snack. Using potato flour is the secret of its wonderful, soft texture.

INGREDIENTS
butter, for greasing
3 eggs, separated
⅜ cup superfine sugar
⅜ cup potato flour
1 cup almonds, blanched, peeled, and chopped finely
finely grated rind of 1 orange
generous ½ cup orange juice
salt
confectioners' sugar, for dusting

Generously grease a round 8-inch/20-cm cake pan. Beat the egg yolks with the sugar in a medium bowl until pale and thick and the mixture leaves a ribbon trail when the whisk is lifted. Stir in the potato flour, almonds, orange rind, and orange juice.

Whisk the egg whites with a pinch of salt in another bowl until stiff. Gently fold the whites into the egg yolk mixture.

Pour the mixture into the pan and bake in a preheated oven, 325°F/160°C, for 50–60 minutes, until golden and just firm to the touch. Turn out onto a cooling rack. Sift over a little confectioners' sugar to decorate before serving.

makes 16 slices | prep 1 hr 15 mins | cook 5 mins

rich chocolate loaf

Another rich chocolate dessert, this loaf is very simple to make and can be served with coffee as well.

INGREDIENTS
5½ oz/150 g semisweet chocolate
6 tbsp unsalted butter
7¼ oz/210 g canned condensed milk
2 tsp cinnamon
2¾ oz/75 g almonds
75 g/2¾ oz amaretti cookies, broken
1¾ oz/50 g dried no-need-to-soak apricots,
  roughly chopped

Line a 1½-lb/675-g loaf pan with a sheet of foil.

Using a sharp knife, roughly chop the almonds into small pieces.

Place the chocolate, butter, milk, and cinnamon in a heavy-bottom pan.

Heat the chocolate mixture over low heat for 3–4 minutes, stirring with a wooden spoon, or until the chocolate has melted. Beat the mixture well.

Stir the almonds, cookies, and apricots into the chocolate mixture, stirring with a wooden spoon, until well mixed.

Pour the mixture into the prepared pan and let chill in the refrigerator for about 1 hour or until set.

Cut the chocolate loaf into slices to serve.

makes 6 slices | prep 15 mins | cook 40 mins

pear & ginger cake

This deliciously buttery pear and ginger cake is ideal with coffee or you can serve it with cream for a delicious dessert.

INGREDIENTS
14 tbsp unsalted butter, softened
6 oz/175 g superfine sugar
175 g/6 oz self-rising flour, sifted
3 tsp ginger
3 eggs, beaten
1 lb/450 g eating pears, peeled,
   cored, and sliced thinly
1 tbsp soft brown sugar

Lightly grease and line the base of a deep 8-inch/20.5-cm cake pan.

Using a whisk, combine 6 oz/175 g of the butter with the sugar, flour, ginger, and eggs and mix to form a smooth consistency.

Spoon the cake mixture into the prepared pan, leveling out the surface.

Arrange the pear slices over the cake mixture. Sprinkle with the brown sugar and dot with the remaining butter.

Bake in a preheated oven, 350°F/180°C, for 35–40 minutes or until the cake is golden and feels springy to the touch.

Serve the pear and ginger cake warm, with ice cream or cream, if you wish.

makes 12–16 slices | prep 10 mins + 20 mins cooling | cook 40 mins

panforte di siena

Chewy, sticky panforte is the traditional Christmas cake of Siena. Chocolate was first added to the recipe when cocoa arrived from the New World and became the fashionable ingredient.

INGREDIENTS
butter, for greasing
¼ cup candied cherries, cut into fourths
⅔ cup mixed candied orange and lemon peel, chopped finely
2 tbsp candied ginger, chopped coarsely
1 cup slivered almonds
¾ cup hazelnuts, toasted and ground coarsely
⅜ cup all-purpose flour
¼ cup unsweetened cocoa
1 tsp ground cinnamon
¼ tsp ground cloves
¼ tsp ground nutmeg
¼ tsp ground coriander
⅓ cup honey
generous ½ cup golden superfine sugar
1 tsp orange flower water
confectioners' sugar, for dusting

VARIATION
You can replace the candied cherries with dried cranberries and the candied ginger with the same amount of candied pineapple.

Preheat the oven to 325°F/160°C. Thoroughly grease the bottom of an 8-inch/20-cm loose-bottom cake or tart pan. Line the bottom with nonstick parchment paper. Place the cherries, candied peel, ginger, almonds, and hazelnuts in a bowl. Sift in the flour, cocoa, cinnamon, cloves, nutmeg, and coriander, and mix. Set aside.

Place the honey, sugar, and orange flower water in a pan and heat gently until the sugar has dissolved. Bring the mixture to a boil and boil steadily until a temperature of 241°F/116°C has been reached on a sugar thermometer, or a small amount of the mixture forms a soft ball when dropped into cold water.

Quickly remove the pan from the heat and stir in the dry ingredients. Mix thoroughly and turn into the prepared pan. Spread evenly and bake in the preheated oven for 30 minutes. Let cool in the pan. Turn out and carefully peel away the lining paper. Dust confectioners' sugar lightly over the top and cut into wedges to serve.

serves 10 | prep 15 mins + 8 hrs chilling | cook 5 mins

italian chocolate christmas pudding

This pudding is a wonderful alternative for anyone who dislikes a traditional Christmas pudding, but there is absolutely no reason why it should be served only at Christmas!

INGREDIENTS
butter, for greasing
½ cup mixed candied fruit, chopped
⅓ cup raisins
grated rind of ½ orange
3 tbsp orange juice
3 tbsp light cream
**12 oz/350 g semisweet
   chocolate, chopped**
½ cup cream cheese
**4 oz/115 g amaretti cookies, broken into
   coarse pieces**
to serve
½ cup whipping cream
2 tbsp amaretto
1 oz/25 g semisweet chocolate, grated

Grease a 3½-cup/850-ml heatproof bowl with butter. Place the candied fruit, raisins, orange rind, and juice in a bowl and mix together. Put the light cream and chocolate in a pan and heat gently until the chocolate has melted. Stir until smooth, then stir in the fruit mixture. Let cool.

Place the cream cheese and a little of the chocolate mixture in a large bowl and beat together until smooth, then stir in the remaining chocolate mixture. Stir in the broken amaretti cookies. Pour into the prepared bowl, cover with plastic wrap, and let chill in the refrigerator overnight.

To serve, turn the pudding out onto a chilled serving plate. Pour the whipping cream into a bowl and add the amaretto. Whip lightly until slightly thickened. Pour some of the cream over the pudding and sprinkle grated chocolate over the top. Serve with the remaining cream.

VARIATION
For a change, substitute the amaretti cookies with crushed graham crackers and replace the amaretto with the same quantity of brandy.

serves 6 | prep 20 mins | cook 0 mins

ricotta ice cream

The ricotta cheese adds a creamy flavor, while the nuts add a crunchy texture to this ice cream, which needs to be chilled in the freezer overnight.

INGREDIENTS
¼ cup pistachio nuts
¼ cup walnuts or pecan nuts
¼ cup toasted chopped hazelnuts
grated rind of 1 orange
grated rind of 1 lemon
2 tbsp crystallized or preserved ginger
2 tbsp candied cherries
¼ cup dried apricots
3 tbsp raisins
1½ cups ricotta cheese
2 tbsp maraschino, amaretto, or brandy
1 tsp vanilla extract
4 egg yolks
½ cup superfine sugar

to decorate
whipped cream
a few candied cherries, pistachio nuts, or mint leaves

Roughly chop the pistachio nuts and walnuts and mix with the toasted hazelnuts, and the orange and lemon rind.

Finely chop the ginger, cherries, apricots, and raisins, and add to the bowl.

Stir the ricotta cheese evenly through the fruit mixture, then beat in the liqueur and vanilla extract.

Put the egg yolks and sugar in a bowl and whisk hard until very thick and creamy— they may be whisked over a pan of gently simmering water to speed up the process. Leave to cool if necessary.

Carefully fold the ricotta mixture evenly through the beaten eggs and sugar until smoothly blended.

Line a 7 x 5-inch/18 x 12-cm loaf pan with a double layer of plastic wrap or parchment paper. Pour in the ricotta mixture, level the top, cover with more plastic wrap or parchment paper and chill in the freezer until firm—at least overnight.

To serve, carefully remove the ice-cream from the pan and peel off the paper. Place on a serving dish and decorate with whipped cream, candied cherries, pistachio nuts, and/or mint leaves. Serve in slices.

serves 4 | prep 15 mins + 5 hrs freezing | cook 6 mins

lemon granita

A delightful end to a meal or a refreshing way to cleanse the palate, granitas are made from slushy ice, so they need to be served very quickly.

INGREDIENTS
3 lemons
¾ cup lemon juice
3½ oz/100 g superfine sugar
2¼ cups cold water

To make lemon granita, finely grate the lemon rind.

Place the lemon rind, lemon juice, and superfine sugar in a pan. Bring the mixture to a boil and let simmer for 5-6 minutes or until thick and syrupy. Leave to cool.

Once cooled, stir in the cold water and pour into a shallow freezer container with a lid.

Freeze the granita for 4–5 hours, stirring occasionally to break up the ice. Serve as a dessert or as a palate cleanser between courses.

VARIATION
To make coffee granita, place 2 tbsp instant coffee and 2 tbsp sugar in a bowl and pour over 2 tbsp hot water, stirring until dissolved. Stir in 2½ cups cold water and 2 tbsp rum or brandy. Pour the mixture into a shallow freezer container with a lid. Freeze for at least 6 hours, stirring occasionally, to create a grainy texture.

serves 4 | prep 10 mins + 1 hr chilling | cook 20 mins

marsala cherries

This is a popular Venetian dish, made with Morello cherries—the variety most widely grown in Italy.

INGREDIENTS
⅝ **cup superfine sugar**
thinly pared rind of 1 lemon
2-inch/5-cm piece of cinnamon stick
1 cup water
1 cup Marsala
2 lb/900 g morello cherries, pitted
⅔ **cup heavy cream**

Put the sugar, lemon rind, cinnamon stick, water, and Marsala in a heavy-bottom pan and bring to a boil, stirring constantly. Reduce the heat and let simmer for 5 minutes. Remove the cinnamon stick.

Add the cherries, cover, and let simmer gently for 10 minutes. Using a slotted spoon, transfer the cherries to a bowl.

Return the pan to the heat and bring to a boil over high heat. Boil for 3–4 minutes, until thick and syrupy. Pour the syrup over the cherries and set aside to cool, then let chill for at least 1 hour.

Whisk the cream until stiff peaks form. Divide the cherries and syrup between 4 individual dishes or glasses, top with the cream, and serve.

VARIATION
Substitute a full-bodied red wine for the Marsala.

makes 40 | prep 20 mins | cook 20 mins

mini florentines

Serve these cookies at the end of a meal with coffee, or arrange in a shallow presentation box for an attractive gift.

INGREDIENTS
⅓ **cup butter**
⅓ **cup superfine sugar**
2 **tbsp golden raisins or raisins**
2 **tbsp candied cherries, chopped**
2 **tbsp crystallized ginger, chopped**
1 **oz/25 g sunflower seeds**
¾ **cup slivered almonds**
2 **tbsp heavy cream**
6 **oz/175 g semisweet chocolate**

Grease and flour 2 cookie sheets or line with parchment paper.

Place the butter in a small pan and heat gently until melted. Add the sugar, stir until dissolved, then bring the mixture to a boil. Remove from the heat and stir in the golden raisins or raisins, cherries, ginger, sunflower seeds, and almonds. Mix well, then beat in the cream.

Place small teaspoons of the fruit and nut mixture on the prepared cookie sheet, allowing plenty of space for the mixture to spread. Bake in a preheated oven, 350°F/180°C, for 10–12 minutes or until light golden in color.

Remove from the oven and, while still hot, use a circular cookie cutter to pull in the edges to form a perfect circle.

Leave to cool and crispen before removing from the cookie sheet.

Melt most of the chocolate and spread it on a sheet of parchment paper. When the chocolate is on the point of setting, place the cookies flat-side down on the chocolate and leave to harden completely.

Cut around the florentines and remove from the parchment paper. Spread a little more chocolate on the coated side of the florentines and use a fork to mark waves in the chocolate. Leave to set. Arrange the florentines on a plate (or in a presentation box for a gift) with alternate sides facing upward. Keep cool.

makes 16 | prep 20 mins | cook 40 mins

chocolate biscotti

These dry cookies are delicious served with black coffee or dessert wine after your evening meal.

INGREDIENTS
1 egg
⅓ cup superfine sugar
1 tsp vanilla extract
1 cup all-purpose flour
½ tsp baking powder
1 tsp ground cinnamon
1¾ oz/50 g semisweet chocolate, chopped roughly
1¾ oz/50 g toasted slivered almonds
1¾ oz/50 g pine nuts

Lightly grease a large cookie sheet.

Whisk the egg, sugar, and vanilla extract in a mixing bowl with an electric mixer until it is thick and pale—ribbons of mixture should trail from the whisk as you lift it.

Sift the flour, baking powder, and cinnamon into a separate bowl, then sift into the egg mixture and fold in gently. Stir in the chocolate, almonds, and pine nuts.

Turn on to a lightly floured counter and shape into a flat log, 9 inches/23 cm long and ¾ inch/1.5 cm wide. Transfer the log to the cookie sheet.

Bake in a preheated oven, 350°F/180°C, for 20–25 minutes or until golden. Remove from the oven and leave to cool for 5 minutes or until firm.

Transfer the log to a cutting board. Using a serrated bread knife, cut the log on the diagonal into slices about ½ inch/1 cm thick and arrange them on the cookie sheet. Cook for 10–15 minutes, turning halfway through the cooking time.

Leave to cool for about 5 minutes, then transfer to a cooling rack to cool completely.

makes 24 | prep 20 mins | cook 15 mins

white chocolate florentines

These attractive jeweled cookies are coated with white chocolate to give them a delicious flavor.

INGREDIENTS
7 oz/200 g butter
8 oz/225 g superfine sugar
4½ oz/125 g walnuts, chopped
4½ oz/125 g almonds, chopped
2 oz/60 g golden raisins, chopped
1 oz/25 g candied cherries,
1 oz/25 g mixed candied peel,
   chopped finely
2 tbsp light cream
8 oz/225 g white chocolate

Line 3–4 cookie sheets with non-stick parchment paper.

Melt the butter over a low heat and then add the sugar, stirring until it has dissolved. Boil the mixture for exactly 1 minute. Remove from the heat.

Add the walnuts, almonds, golden raisins, candied cherries, candied peel, and cream to the pan, stirring well to mix.

Drop heaped teaspoonfuls of the mixture onto the cookie sheets, allowing plenty of room for the cookies to spread while cooking. Bake in a preheated oven, 350°F/180°C, for 10 minutes or until golden brown.

Remove the cookies from the oven and neaten the edges with a knife while they are still warm. Leave to cool slightly, and then transfer them to a cooling rack to cool completely.

Melt the chocolate in a heatproof bowl placed over a pan of gently simmering water. Spread the underside of the cookies with chocolate and use a fork to make wavy lines across the surface. Let cool completely.

Store the Florentines in an airtight tin, kept in a cool place.

makes 20 | prep 5 mins + 1 hr chilling | cook 5 mins

italian chocolate truffles

These are flavored with almonds and chocolate, and are simplicity itself to make. Served with coffee, they are the perfect end to a meal.

INGREDIENTS
6 oz/175 g semisweet chocolate
2 tbsp amaretto or
   orange-flavored liqueur
3 tbsp unsalted butter
1¾ oz/50 g confectioners' sugar
½ cup ground almonds
1¾ oz/50 g grated milk chocolate

Melt the chocolate with the liqueur in a heatproof bowl set over a pan of hot water, stirring until well combined.

Add the butter and stir until it has melted. Stir in the confectioners' sugar and the ground almonds.

Leave the mixture in a cool place until firm enough to roll into 24 balls.

Place the grated chocolate on a plate and roll the truffles in the chocolate to coat them.

Place the truffles in paper candy cases and chill for at least 1 hour.